The Cherokee Full Circle

THE CHEROKEE FULL CIRCLE

A Practical Guide to Ceremonies and Traditions

J. T. GARRETT and
MICHAEL TLANUSTA GARRETT

Bear & Company
Rochester, Vermont

Bear & Company
One Park Street
Rochester, Vermont 05767
www.InnerTraditions.com

Bear & Company is a division of Inner Traditions International

Library of Congress Cataloging-in-Publication Data
Garrett, J. T., 1942–
    The Cherokee full circle : a practical guide to ceremonies and
traditions / J. T. Garrett, Michael Tlanusta Garrett.
       p. cm.
    ISBN 978-187918195-3
    1. Cherokee Indians—Religions. 2. Cherokee Indians—Medi-
cine. 3. Indians of North America—Religion. 4. Indians of North
America—Medicine. I. Garrett, Michael Tlanusta, 1970- II. Title.

E99.C5 G23 2002
299'.7855—dc21

                          2002074486

Printed and bound at Lake Book Manufacturing

10 9 8 7 6

Text design by Priscilla Baker

This book was typeset in Legacy Serif, with Neuland and Frutiger as
display fonts

Contents

Introduction

*In the old days, there was peace and harmony in the
mountains where our people (the Cherokee) lived, struggled
for survival, and raised the young ones. There was respect
for the elders, and they were honored in our ceremonies.
Don't get me wrong, we were not without our difficulties,
'cause there were plenty with just surviving a winter in the
mountains. We were a people who shared all things, and we
did not own the land. It and we were free to be responsible
to care for others who also shared. We had everything in
nature, and Mother Earth gifted us with plants for food
and for our ills. We beat our drum, sang our songs, danced,
and worked for survival of the family, clan, and tribe. We
were one with each other and the Universal Circle of Life.*

—OSCAR ROGERS,
CHEROKEE ELDER,
EASTERN BAND OF CHEROKEE INDIANS

From the dawn of time, human existence has borne witness to
people banding together in the face of adversity for the sake
of survival. Mutual protection and support were the function
of relational bonds that have historically held people together
under a common purpose. Individual survival rooted itself in
the survival and well-being of the group. Essentially, survival
required independence based on the interdependence of each
person within the group. Although the hardships facing many

1

people today are different from those of our ancestors, both in kind and magnitude, one common fact remains: *people need people.*

The traditional customs of Native Americans originated not only as a means of survival in response to the demands of difficult conditions, but also in response to the various needs that comprise what it means to be human. Native Americans have existed for thousands of years, developing a rich heritage that exemplifies the value of the group. The cultural practices and traditional views that arose out of a need to survive are for many Native Americans a way of life profoundly rooted in a pride and respect for such a gift—the gift of life.

Today it is estimated that there are more than 2.5 million Native Americans living in the United States, and this population is steadily growing. Although Native Americans account for only about 1 percent of the total U.S. population, they have been described as comprising 50 percent of the diversity that exists in this country. This diversity among Native American nations is illustrated by 250 languages and 500 or more federally recognized tribes, and some 400 state-recognized tribes in the United States today. The diversity is also seen in varying levels of cultural commitment among the members of a given tribe or nation. However, a prevailing sense of "Indianness" based on a common worldview seems to bind Native Americans together as a people of many peoples.

Being Indian is not just the degree of American Indian blood one may have, but a way of life and a connection to the ancestors that taught us to live and be Indian. As a Cherokee elder said, "You are not Cherokee because you have a BIA [Bureau of Indian Affairs] enrollment card. You have to live and be the culture that is based on a unique heritage. You have to know what it means to gift with the sacred tobacco and how to give thanks to the Great One each day. It is a way of life with values that are uniquely Cherokee."

As federally recognized, the proper and legal definition of an Indian is a person of American Indian or Alaska Native descent. However, people of most tribes prefer to be called by their own traditional and/or accepted names, such as the Cherokee, Catawba, Seneca, Seminole, and so forth. "Native American," which is acceptable, has become more inclusive of state-recognized and other tribal peoples who may be seeking recognition as natives who trace their ancestry back to the time here before the Europeans arrived in North America.

It is also important to note that many Americans have some Indian blood and may not be "recognized" as American Indian or Native Americans, but they are certainly of Indian ancestry. As an elder said, "Call me what you want, just call me to dinner." However, he said, "Deep down inside, I really don't like being called 'Indian' per se because it was used in a negative way when I was going to the public school off the reservation." He also reminded me that the word *squaw* was a negative word, and that he remembered feeling angry when someone referred to an Indian girl as a squaw.

In this book we will use American Indian and Native American, or refer to the specific tribe when appropriate. As Doc Sequoyah has said, "I am a Cherokee first, a Bigcove Cherokee second, and I even got a little German in me, but I am an American Indian."

American Indian traditional values consist of sharing, co-operation, noninterference, being, family and tribe, harmony with nature, a time orientation toward living in the present, preference for explanation of a natural phenomena with the supernatural, and a deep respect for elders. In contrast, American mainstream values emphasize domination, competition, aggression, doing, individualism and the nuclear family, mastery over nature, saving and greed, a time orientation toward living for the future, a preference for scientific explanation of things, and reverence of youth. We, the authors, followed the ways of our grandmothers and grandfathers as Cherokee Indians who have lived in the region of North Carolina and Tennessee for many generations. Having an Irish father and grandfather has helped to make the differences between the cultures more clear. While one is not better than the other, there are certainly differences that caused some confusion while growing up on and off the reservation.

Native Americans have always stressed the importance of cultural ways and traditions as taught by the elders from our ancestors. Attitudes and behaviors associated with various Native American values can be expressed as follows.

VALUES, ATTITUDES, AND BEHAVIORS

In a group, **harmony** is the focus, which discourages boisterous individual behavior. At the same time, **autonomy** is respected. When I (J. T.) was young we were taught not to interfere with someone for fear that we would "take on their consequences."

It is important to demonstrate that one has the ability to use keen abilities of hearing, seeing, and smelling; these were of critical importance for the tribe in earlier years, for developing hunting and fishing skills as well as for finding plants for Medicine and protecting the family during travels. Our grandfather was a great tracker, a skill that was admired by many. Also, his keen ability of **observation** was well known, along with his patience. These are honored traits and learned abilities in the group setting.

Respect is honored and disrespect is shunned within the tribe. Respect for the elders shows strength and humility, which is greatly honored. Also respect for nature, the animals, the winged ones, and every living creature is honored as demonstrating sacredness. Earlier relationships demonstrated harmony and respect for nature to the point that "even moving a rock without asking permission showed disrespect."

The **spiritual** ways are emphasized today as they always have been, since there was an understanding with Mother Earth, Father Sky, Sun, Moon, and all of the natural environment called the Universal Circle. The Great One was thanked for everything provided for life survival. The elders are a resource of wisdom and a source of learning the "old ways" for survival.

Still today, despite searching on computers and so many resources available, the elder is treated as the Beloved Man and the Beloved Woman in the tribe, who is the most wise about all things. There is a certain **caution** with newcomers and with new relationships. Also, personal and family issues are "kept within the family circle, not to be hung out like laundry for everyone to see."

Before the advent of television, storytelling provided many of the lessons learned, as well as guidance on values and behaviors expected as members of the tribe. Traditional American Indian values and attitudes include a sense of humor that can only be appreciated because of living that culture and time, as is the case with other cultures of people. In growing up we called them "Indian jokes," only because you had to be American Indian or Cherokee to understand the joke. Humor is important in the bonding process of a family and with friends, "as long as it's proper and does not criticize anybody else," as Mother and Grandmother would say.

The key to American Indian values, attitudes, and behaviors is to be strong and endure while belonging to a group, while respecting nature, the elders, the family, and the tribe. The focus is on being a protector and helper while honoring the traditions and cultural ways with respect and dignity.

American Indian "ways" can be misconstrued by the dominate population when he or she does *not stare or look directly at a person*. The idea of "you look at me when I talk to you" would be just the reverse in a traditional American Indian family. The reason for looking down is to show respect and "not to interfere with the person as you show respect." An important value is to demonstrate **modesty,** which demonstrates humility. Loud behavior and getting attention is not respected by others. As the reader will see in reading this book, **belonging** is an important value. In earlier years, belonging to a family and tribe would assure your survival, compared to the popular notion today of "making it on your own." Showing **patience** and **silence** were virtues of self-control and inner strength admired by American Indians. **Listening** and **moderation** show diligence and respect for the storyteller, the family, visitors, or within the tribe in general. We did not want to embarrass our family or tribe. Unlike pushing a student to speak out and to be aggressive with answers, this type of behavior was frowned upon. The elders would call this type of behavior to our attention.

In 1879, when Richard H. Pratt founded one of the first Indian boarding schools and proposed his remarkable slogan "Kill the Indian and save the man!" he could not have grasped the depth and breadth of wisdom offered by Native American values and practices. Through value consensus Native Americans have consistently resisted acculturation into mainstream society possibly more than any other ethnic minority group. Pratt did understand one fundamental principle underlying the idea of assimilation: break the spirit of a people and you have broken the people. However, he could not have foreseen the vigor and tenacity of the Native American spirit, which has survived, nearly as long as Mother Earth herself, on the sacred views and traditions of its peoples. As a Cherokee elder said, "We have never wanted to be a part of their [white man's] group, so why didn't they just leave us alone?" Another elder said, "However things go we are part of the past, and we are the future. Instead of dwelling on the 'wrongs' of the past we must be the example of 'rights' for the future."

FULL CIRCLE TEACHINGS

There has been little opportunity for the public to participate in forums or gatherings with American Indian Elders, especially Medicine Men (and Women). The traditional teachings, or "Medicine-way," has been gradually lost with the changing culture of indigenous people in America. As one elder said in 1984, "It is time for us to renew our cultural ways so the young people will not forget. We have lost too much, and in one generation we could lose it all." The tribes have initiated cultural programs in schools and in their communities, as well as started teaching the language. Multicultural programs were started at universities and many programs were started to bridge the generational gap. (The difficulty is always procuring the funding to keep these programs going.) However, little was available for those outside the tribes who were interested in learning more about the traditional teachings.

There is concern within the tribes about sharing teachings that might be considered sacred. Who can blame any American Indian tribe for being skeptical of federal monies for them to share their cultural traditions or have university studies done on the existing culture? In addition, there is so little in the literature on traditional beliefs and Indian Medicine, and much of what is out there is written by non-Indians. From our perspective, we are glad there is some really good information provided, but how can it be framed in a way that is useful for survival in our society and for our way of life today?

We, the authors, decided to start a weekend workshop called Full Circle gatherings to provide teachings based on traditional and cultural ways of the Cherokee and other American Indian tribal ways. These gatherings are held on the Cherokee Indian reservation, where we are comfortable with the indoor and outdoor setting for having group and full participation. The Full Circle gatherings, to which participants are personally invited, is an opportunity for Cherokee and other elders to participate in sharing cultural teachings.

A typical Full Circle gathering starts on a Friday evening and sets the stage with drumming, flute music, and a traditional smudge using sage and cedar as a "clearing-way." There is time for setting the weekend agenda while bonding as a circle group. There is always a traditional story and song-chants with the drumming to remind us somewhat of what this gathering must have been in earlier years. This is a teaching time that draws educators, counselors, ministers, energy workers, and others interested in learning more about what is sometimes called the "old wisdom," and simply to enjoy the teachings and outside activities. We have been hosting Full Circle gatherings twice a year for the past nine years.

Full Circle becomes a family, in a sense, as we enjoy and look forward to the time to come together, similar to a family reunion. It is also a time to "let our hair down" or "confront ourselves" or to "have a reality check," as described by participants. It is also a time to enjoy the healing energy of Mother Earth or to "feel protected while renewing our lives to deal with the stress of work and family at home." The focus is on adults, primarily because of space and at the request of adults who attend. We utilize leaders that are trained counselors, called "helpers," to facilitate groups for activities and exercises.

Full Circle brings us back to nature with outside trips and exercises that focus on getting back in touch with the energy of nature. It also includes discussion of plants as "helpers" for healing, as well as techniques that will be discussed in this book for reframing our lives and healing in a group setting. Sunday morning is a time for ceremony—the healing circle— and a time of reflection as we have a "clearing-way" to help guide the journey home.

The events of 9/11, the terrorist attack on America that left the World Trade towers in New York in rubble, has changed us as free-spirited Americans. As a friend says, "The giant has awakened, and he is jealous of the golden harp and golden egg. The resentment of others for our wealth and privilege will mean that we put up gates to protect our property." This enemy is not so clearly defined and easily seen. The events of September 11th have also brought people to Full Circle who want to know about the traditional teachings of earlier American Indians for survival. Many of the techniques and exercises that we use have more validity today, it seems, than ever before. As a Cherokee elder put it, "We will be all right, although it may not seem that way right now. We are survivors who always look to our ancestors for the right ways and for survival. It is time to renew the lessons of the past to bridge the future. It is even more important that we remind ourselves that our purpose here is to be a protector of Mother Earth and a helper to all living things."

Full Circle gatherings have dusted off some older techniques and exercises to be "helpers" with relationships and healing. Several of those are presented in this book. The traditional idea of life being a continual "beginning-again" is a wonderful lesson, as are teachings that involve doing things or just being in nature. It is a time of "a new spring," as an elder put it, a time when life begins again with the blooming of flowers, and bees and birds enjoy spreading the seeds of life as we listen to them sing. We must not forget the enjoyment of life, while we muddle in the mud wrong-doing and wrong-being. Nature is our lesson and our answer to harmony and balance. We must bring back the drumming, the old songs, and the dance that lifts our spirits. We must listen to our ancestors and honor our elders as we relearn respect for each other. Instead of taking time to smell the roses, we'd best take time to plant the roses.

The teachings of Full Circle bring the traditional ways of American Indian wisdom to us for use in our lives. The East is the Path of enlightenment. The Sun rises in the East; it is the fire that warms our hearts and fuels our beginning as a spirit coming into this world. We look to family for protection and for support, and we establish an extended family of friends to encourage and to support our feelings. We want to be where we feel we belong. We look to the South as the Path of Innocence and Spirit where we are connected to Mother Earth. Like our youth, we will master our circumstances for survival. We look to the West as the Path of Introspection for us to continually look within and at ourselves for strength, and endurance for independence. The flow of energy is like water that is the life blood. We turn to the North as the Path of Quiet and Truth for us to learn the lessons that have swept the Universal Circle through the winds of time. We learn generosity as we give of our gifts for the benefit of all living things here on Mother Earth.

This is our Medicine Wheel to protect our way of life, our culture, our traditions, and our future survival. These lessons of our ancestors teach us to honor our elders, teach our children respect, and bring us peace.

Full Circle teachings are a combination of the two generations of father and son, but with many generations of "old wisdom" of Native American traditional teachings and techniques backing us up. Many of the ideas described in this book represent generations of stories and cultural traditions passed down through time in order that the spirit of Indian people may continue to survive and to thrive. By understanding cultural differences we are able to recognize themes of commonality that exist for all cultures, for each of us as individual human beings. As a Cherokee elder put it, "To understand the Medicine of life is to understand your own purpose for being human beings."*

---

*The term Medicine as it is used here is intended to be much broader than *medicine* is used today. Medicine is a term, familiar within all tribes, that refers to everything in the Circle of Life that influences an American Indian and Alaska Native way of life. While it is referred to by some tribes as Medicine Bundle, the term Medicine describes physical, mental, spiritual, and natural aspects of life that are connected and interrelated. Also, in this text the terms American Indian and Native American are used interchangeably, but many Indians prefer to be known by their tribal name or as American Indians and Alaska Natives.

Full Circle utilizes the group as one of the primary settings in which healing may occur. There are many advantages to using the group for this process of personal transformation. For instance, some of the benefits include the lifelike quality that a group adds to the process and the value of the support and input provided by others who may be experiencing similar issues or concerns. For Native Americans, the group is an ideal place and way for learning, for transition, and for expressing personal growth. Connection and support play a prominent role in healing and in wellness. For this reason, Native American traditional practices and ceremonies emphasize the importance of the group.

The idea of the group is rooted in all societies and all cultures; though it may serve differing functions and be valued in diverse ways. Similarly, vast differences exist both within and between cultural groups concerning values, beliefs, and practices. The fact that one cultural group may be different from another has spurred great attempts at defining, examining, explaining, expounding upon, and, in some cases, accommodating those differences. Truly, there are differences between groups just as there are differences between individuals. Differences among peoples should be understood and welcomed based on the premise that *it is better to resolve differences than to live with indifference.*

Quite possibly, it is through our differences that we learn the true value of that which makes us one. We all have different worldviews. We all have slightly different perspectives on what we see, what we hear, and what we experience. Still, we also share something very sacred, and something that sometimes is forgotten or neglected in the search for a meaningful grasp of the world as we know it. All cultures seem to understand that our differences offer an opportunity and appreciation for the wonderful world we live in today. However, while some of us want to better understand and appreciate the uniqueness of other cultures of people, some prefer to be biased, and they are all right with that. As an elder teacher said, "It is all right to be different, one to another. The traditional Indian view is to accept differences as a way of life, and that is okay. It has been difficult for us as Cherokees to understand why others could not just accept us as we accepted them. Of course, I believe this nonacceptance and tendency to interfere is universal with some all over the world. While we cannot change the world, we can certainly accept acceptance within our own hearts."

It is the ever-challenging job of the helper to draw on this sacred strength, the humanity inherent within all of us, to enter a person's frame of reference and to understand before attempting to walk the path of healing with that person. In the traditional teachings a helper plays a very important role in every aspect of the American Indian and Alaska Native life. One of the first teachings learned as a very young child is to be a helper, to help Grandmother in order to learn respect for the elders, or to be a helper to learn skills of planting, then to learn the skills of hunting as you grow older. The helper is also the person who guides and protects you as you develop to a point when you yourself will be a helper. This development is emphasized in the Full Circle gatherings, where helpers are utilized in every activity and exercise, teaching as participants evolve in learning the Medicine-way of life.

We must not forget that we all have this sacred power and that we are all a part of one another. Finally, we must keep in mind that no one is better equipped to change someone than that someone. Patience and respect are invaluable tools for any form of healing. The Cherokee elders have taught us that there is healing in calmness and strength in humility. The lesson of perspective is utterly crucial to working with anyone who is different from ourselves. It is always important to remember that no two people have exactly the same experiences; we are all different, and in a sense, possess what could be considered a "personal culture" of our own. Yet our humanity lends us common ground for experiencing and for relating to one another. Ultimately, in seeking wellness, we must not forget to relate to ourselves, always keeping in touch with our inner experience. It is important for all cultures to resolve our difference and avoid the conflicts of indifference.

FULL CIRCLE: THE PREMISE

Although the work presented here originates from the traditions and practices of a diverse and proud people, and although the techniques are constructed by Native Americans, the ideas and the methods of application are universal in scope. *Full Circle* is an introduction to the traditional framework of healing and growth for use by both Native Americans and non-Native Americans alike. Indeed, people are people, and what you find if you take the time to look is this: *People are more alike than different when it comes to the human spirit. Full Circle* should be read and practiced with this thought in mind.

The teachings presented herein offer techniques and ways of thinking that are helpful to us as individuals, as well as in the group setting. Native American teachings inherently possess certain universal truths that apply to each of us. Perspective is the key, and the message is clear: Our humanity is our commonality—we must use it, and use it well.

To avoid confusion, the term "Full Circle" will be used throughout this book to encompass the concepts and teachings of American Indian wisdom that are sometimes difficult to describe because of cultural differences and references that are not within much of our grasp today as a society and culture. Our purpose in describing these teachings and techniques is to frame them for understanding today, as well as to preserve this wonderful Old Wisdom. The weekend gathering that we host twice a year will be referred to in this book as Full Circle gathering.

Full Circle is a concept describing in each of us the cyclical nature of self-knowledge (knowing), harmony and balance (being), and life purpose (doing) for maintaining harmony or recognizing sources of disharmony. It is based on the premise that wellness depends upon the conscious and continuous interaction of these three components. Spiraling to a higher level of awareness seems to occur when we cross over into a different frame of mind and of being. Traditional Indian techniques used sacred objects or places that would set the stage for this transformation. Therefore, using the circle or group was a powerful way to bring people together for council, healing, and spiritual activities.

Just as life itself follows a spiral motion that moves us through our development, Full Circle embodies the realm of our life and its constant motion. This book utilizes traditional and natural ways of Indian people to get us back in touch with ourselves. The circle becomes something more powerful than just people sitting around simply talking; it becomes a place for healing and continued wellness.

THE FULL CIRCLE LEADER

American Indians use the terms *leader* and *helper* somewhat differently than other cultures do today. The traditional leader was someone with strong spiritual abilities who would encourage others to be involved and participate in being a helper to others. The leader was often the teacher or the Medicine Man. The leader could be the person working in the planting field, a person of humility, and a person who might have less in terms of wealth as we know it today. It was most likely not someone who is appointed or commissioned to accomplish something. The leader or helper becomes an integral part of the Full Circle gathering by allowing the opportunity for a group to be guided. The leader may be a mental, physical, natural, or spiritual healer who provides some form of guidance to the group. The most important qualification for this role is that the person be a natural leader.

What is a leader, anyway? Is a leader not someone who either makes choices or helps in the making of choices? If so, then we are all leaders in our own lives. As we will discuss later in chapter 1, the intrinsic value of "leadership" is valued over any specific title or role.

The exercises presented herein provide ways of receiving information or guidance, both in the group and within the individual. A leader may be a healer or one who is in need of self-healing. In order to help others we must be able and willing to help ourselves. In order to help others take a look at themselves, we must be willing to look at ourselves. Ultimately we must not ask others to do what we ourselves would not be willing to do, and even then we must do so with respect and patience. In a traditional sense, openness is the key to an awareness of oneself within the greater Universal Circle.

The leader often becomes a "helper" in the process of healing or finding a path to wellness through balance and harmony. Attaining balance becomes the process of "grounding," and achieving harmony becomes the process of bonding with all things around us in our environment. Therefore, everything becomes a helper to us. This includes plants, animals, minerals, birds, Mother Earth, trees, rocks, and everything having a purpose in our lives. Nothing should be overlooked. In this way, one can see why it was important for Indians to give thanks to the Great One for everything. The leader could also be a support person, such as a trusted elder or a friend, until the individual becomes a leader in her or his own vision; then that elder or friend becomes the leader. The value of leadership within Native American culture will be discussed in more detail in chapter 1.

Full Circle provides dialogue and techniques emphasizing wellness and healing rather than illness and disharmony. Anyone who seeks with an openness in their search will find answers to their difficulties. It takes a special willingness to seek out truth, regardless of how difficult it may seem. The traditional stories told by the Indian elders and teachers usually guide rather than direct answers to situations. As an example, there is a Cherokee story about the Medicine Elders and other special persons coming together in the mountains during certain times of the year to seek the Medicine together. For several evenings they would dance and use their rattles and drums with chants and songs, sharing stories of their experiences and journeys during that year. They all knew that they were there for a purpose, and they knew that during the last evening of their circle together, the "spirit people" would place something very special in their Medicine bag. This represents something they would learn, such as a new use for an herb, or a story that could be used, or possibly some special ability, or a healing power they would receive in order to help others. It might be something broad, or it could be something very specific for bringing about harmony and balance in their world.

As community groups come together to solve problems for the benefit of the community, traditional circle gatherings would be used for "healing of the towns and state of affairs," as an elder put it. Today it is not always the case that our most humble and caring people are our leaders. It is more likely that the most vocal and affluent are our leaders. Full Circle teaches us to be patient when we have something to say and to say something out of patience, rather than being driven to accomplish something. Calm resolve and guidance by helpers of various aspects of our community can bring about change in subtle ways, as long as we can leave out the egos and emotional issues. The leaders help to "work through those emotions and act within the laws of the tribe to bring about resolve. We start by thanking the Great One, calling in our ancestors for guidance, and sharing the pipe of peace symbolically while we bring in the helpers to work together for the good of all," says an elder. In that sense, there is healing.

Now it is your time to enter the circle and to seek your own path to wellness as a leader, helper, and healer of humankind and Mother Earth.

PART ONE
Traditional Ways

1
Cultural Values and Traditional Views

One day, many years ago, when I (J.T.) was still a little one, I was sitting with my grandfather by the edge of the Oconaluftee River. He was sitting on a rock enjoying the afternoon sun while I was playing in the water. "What do you see?" he asked me.

"I see the water," I said.

"What else do you see?" he asked.

"Well, I see the fish," I answered, because there were little minnows swimming around in the water.

"What else do you see?" he asked.

"I see the rock," I said.

"What else do you see?" he asked again.

"Well, I don't see anything else." I answered.

"No," he said, "What you see is a reflection of the whole world before you."

Culture is born from beliefs and traditions that draw people together with a sense of "oneness" through the unity of family, clan, and tribe. Traditional views shape Native American assessments of meaning for any given situation. Working with people sometimes requires an understanding of the very basic beliefs and values that drive a culture before attempting to "step inside their skin" for working toward change. By better understanding differences, we are better able to understand common themes that affect all of our lives.

Just as a reminder, traditional American Indians in earlier years focused on the tribe first, the clan second, and the family third in terms of importance and duty. As an elder put it, "It was just one of those things you understood in growing up: our tribe came first and the individual came last. That was the way we survived." The family was the centrality of the circle, with all things in our immediate environment being in harmony and balance. The individual was simply not allowed to upset the order of the family traditionally. To be ostracized from the family because of bad deeds or acts of disturbance of the family order was to be exposed to the elements for survival. The centrality of the family in harmony and balance was critically paramount for survival of the family, clan, and tribe.

CENTRALITY OF FAMILY

Because Native American culture is one in which the survival of the individual is synonymous with that of the community, the family holds a prominent place. However, "family" extends well beyond one's immediate relatives to extended family relatives, members of one's clan, members of the community, all other living creatures in this world, nature as a whole, and the universe itself.

What mainstream defines as "family" takes on a much broader view with Native Americans. Family relationships include much more than the biological connections of the nuclear family. For example, the claiming of non-blood relatives or "fictive kin" as family members is commonly practiced. Traditional beliefs allow us to think that "being Indian" is not about the blood that flows in your veins, but how you live in a cultural and traditional way in respecting the sacredness of the American Indian way of life.

The structural characteristics of the extended family network and tribal network function as facilitators of social responsibility, reciprocity, and value transmission. Indian perceptions of family are universal in scope.

Traditionally, it is the primary responsibility of the grandparents to raise the children, and that of the parents to provide economic support. Child rearing is thought to encompass too important a responsibility for young parents, who are, in the eyes of the elders, not yet wise enough to handle such an important task. Thus, the value placed on the roles to be fulfilled by the elders becomes apparent. In addition, the participation of others (aunts, uncles, brothers, sisters, valued friends) in the extended family and community network adds emphasis to the sense of unity that is experienced in the centrality of the group.

For Native Americans, "family" symbolizes a unique approach to the process of living. The entire universe is thought of as "a family" with each and every one of its members serving a useful and necessary function. In the traditional way, elders direct the children's attention outward to the things with which they coexist (trees, plants, animals, the land). In this way, Native American children develop a heightened level of sensitivity for everything of which they are a part, for the cyclical motion of life, and for the customs and traditions of their people. As an elder said, "We are all kin to every living being."

The presence of "interdependence" is well understood and experienced. The animals are thought of as our "four-legged" brothers and sisters; the Earth is our Mother; the sky, Father;

the Moon, Grandmother; and the Sun, Grandfather to all living creatures. The connection we all have with others can be considered nothing short of sacred. For Native Americans, relation is something that extends beyond that of biological connection to one of a more spiritual nature. As the elder said, "Every cell in our body is connected to every part of the universal cell or Circle of Life. We (American Indians) believe this connection is also with our ancestors in spirit."

In the traditional teachings family was everything, but even family did not come before tribe as the larger family. Mother Earth in the traditional teachings is our Universal Mother who gives us life, and Father Sky represents that part of the Universal Circle that sustains life. We come into this life from the center of existence, greeting the Sun as an "apportioner," a provider. The family of the East protects us as we spiral toward the South as a child, being guided to learn as Mother Earth and nature cradle our self-mastery. We spiral to the West as we learn to compete and develop dependence under the watchful eye of Grandmother Moon. The spiral continues as an adult, where we learn generosity as we gain wisdom. Father Sky provides the winds of power and time, which spirals us as we become an elder with true wisdom and move to East, protected by our family, until we begin again.

LEADERSHIP

Leadership is nurtured by focusing on self-mastery, inner strength, and the development of individual abilities. Kindness, generosity, autonomy, noninterference, and sharing are all ideals held in high reverence by Native American culture. Young children are taught these values and the importance of

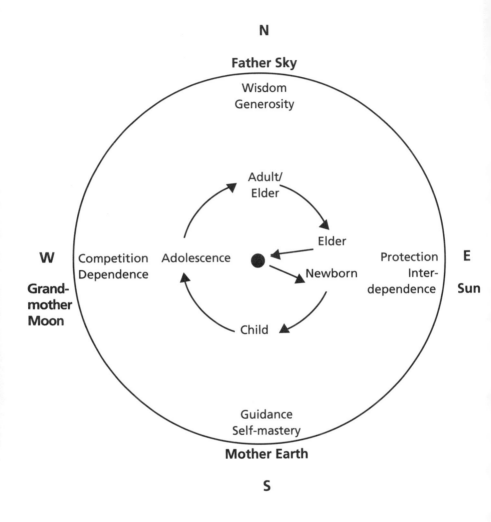

In the Universal Circle everything is related and connected to everything else in the creation of life.

community from a very early age. It is necessary that traditional roles be embraced for the traditional values to be preserved in the minds and hearts of the people.

Through guidance offered by the elders, appropriate ways of acting and interacting are handed down through stories and sacred rituals that reveal the secrets to a Native American way of life. This lifestyle is grounded in the practice of harmony within oneself, with others, and with one's surroundings. For everything that is taken, something is given in return. Such views emphasize what is considered honorable behavior in the eyes of the community, and thus form the foundation for Native American leadership. Kindness and respect are not simply ways of acting, but ways of living and feeling. These, in turn, shape the individual to whom others look for leadership.

In emphasizing spiritual and humanistic qualities, Native American views of leadership describe the respected person as the one who acts in the most friendly, generous, considerate, and modest way. To bring attention to oneself for the sake of praise is shameful, especially at the expense of others. Group needs are highly prized as a reflection of a person-oriented rather than task-oriented society. However, every person is expected to be self-defining and thus valued in his or her own right. Therefore, the best leader is the one who listens to every person who offers an opinion and carefully considers all that is said, for every thought counts in the sacred circle.

Traditionally, decisions by the Native American group involve the holding of discussions until a consensus can be reached; only then will action be taken. In this way no one's thoughts are to be overlooked, and a leader is only as strong as the cooperation among his or her people. This agreement represents a strengthening of the harmony through which leaders act to the benefit of their people.

PRINCIPLE OF NONINTERFERENCE

The true significance of a Native American approach to relationships lies in the balance struck between an all-encompassing sense of belonging with one's people and the practice of noninterference. The highest form of respect for another person is respecting his or her natural right to self-determination. This means not interfering (unless asked to do so) with another person's ability to choose, even when it is to keep that person from doing something foolish or dangerous. Noninterference means caring in a respectful way.

Traditionally it would have been considered an insult to the family and tribe for someone to interfere or to show impatience or nonrestraint when another member or a nonmember of the tribe was acting out or causing conflict. Getting into a fight or being aggressive are good examples. As youngsters, we were told to walk away and not to be part of a conflict. In the outside world of assertiveness and aggressiveness this may be looked at as weakness. As an elder said, "Think about it, do you see Indian children making scenes in stores like you do other children? A traditionally raised child is taught patience and not to make a scene in public." It is a challenge to teach this traditional lesson to people today, who have been taught to "speak out" or be aggressive to "get ahead." Ironically, participants at the Full Circle gatherings seem to enjoy this lesson, which leads to much calmer group sessions with much less stress.

The traditional teaching to "just walk away" works in groups as well. It is understood that one can walk away with permission of the group when something bothers them or affects their emotions to the point of upsetting them. They can take a break, and the group will not follow them out or express concern but will allow them time for composure. When they return they are accepted by the leader of the group with a slight head shake. There is no need to interfere by asking what is wrong or by offering solutions. Respect for another dictates that when a person is ready to share information, he will do so. Likewise, if a person is in need of assistance or advice, he will ask. Patience is a Native American virtue. Noninterference basically asserts that caring and respect are not one in the same, but that both are required for harmonious relations with others. One of the highest forms of caring for another person comes through the expression of respect, that is, respecting a person's right and ability to choose for herself, and practicing the patience to allow her to do just that. This respect could be as simple as asking permission before touching someone. As demonstrated in the "Personal Distance" exercise in part 3 (p. 174), the effect of this gesture can be significant. The same philosophy applies to an individual's relation with nature, in which permission must be asked before taking and thanks must be expressed by giving back in some way. This could be as simple as a small prayer giving thanks. It is not too much to ask, yet it makes a world of difference. Thus, noninterference plays a central role in the all-important harmony by which Native Americans live. As an elder said, "To interfere is to take on that energy and to possibly cause problems for yourself and your family. It is better to be a helper with the person making choices, but to let her resolve her own issue." In other words, don't allow yourself to become part of the conflict or interfere, just be a helper.

PURPOSE OF LIFE

Native Americans believe that every life is a gift to be treated with gratitude and respect. What has been referred to as the Harmony Ethic guides much of Native American living. For the Cherokee this encompasses the conscious avoidance of interpersonal conflict in an attempt to maintain reciprocally harmonious relations with all members of the tribe. For instance, the practice of using a neutral third person in the resolution of conflict is a common strategy for traditional Native American culture. The Switching and Split-self exercises in part 3 (pp. 165 and 170) exemplify this strategy.

Incorporating the Principle of Noninterference, the Harmony Ethic is a system based upon caring for fellow human beings through the expression of deep respect. This is the way to achieve harmonious survival. It also involves the presence of individual choice. To the Cherokee, a person has just as much choice in creating harmony as in creating disharmony.

Within the Native American tradition it is widely believed that every person has a purpose to fulfill during his or her lifetime. Every person, like every animal, tree, plant, and mineral, possesses some unique quality or talent to be discovered through a variety of experiences in this world. Harmony is the key to meaningful life experiences in which all learning contributes to an overall life purpose. This purpose is manifested by a striving for the wisdom and generosity exemplified by the Native American elder who has accumulated a lifetime's worth of experience in the world. Our elders have learned the inner secrets to a harmonious existence and are the keepers of this wisdom.

Traditional wisdom tells us that it is our purpose to face the world with courage in our hearts. This courage signifies a

Harmony in Life: Everything on Mother Earth
is part of the song and dance of life.

deep respect for the gift that we have been given through the ability to live, as well as a respect for all life. Courage transcends any circumstance, and ultimately comes from a harmony within oneself and between oneself and one's universe—an inner strength derived from the unity of body, mind, nature, and spirit. There is an old saying: All that moves is sacred—only by understanding this can you realize the rhythm of Mother Earth, and thereby know how to place your feet.

2
Sacred Ceremonies and Traditions

Earlier American Indian ceremonies and gatherings focused on tradition and heritage with games, food, and all the things that bring a community of people together. There are some activities from these old ceremonies that we use in Full Circle to capture these wonderful ways and to apply them today for healing in our lives. Each of the ceremonies had certain activities for learning about the use of plants and foods, skills in game and hunting, and enjoyable competition. This is kept alive in the Fall Festival held in October of each year in Cherokee, North Carolina. However, many activities have been lost with the advent of television and families not getting together as much for resolution of problems and simple entertainment.

In this chapter we share some of the traditions and activities that can have a profound influence on our lives, such as considering a change of name and a change of our way of daily living. The old mask ceremony is a way for us to realize that we do put a mask on for various occasions. What if we still had one ceremony each year in which we could change our mask or take it off, so to speak, and just be who we really want to be inside?

In Native American traditions ceremony is an essential way of connecting with that which is sacred, remembering always our place in the greater Universal Circle. In order to better understand some of the activities and techniques used in Full Circle it is important to look at the origins of ceremonies that have existed for hundreds, even thousands, of years in the hearts and minds of native peoples. It is a way of life that is honored and preserved. It becomes a "giveaway" and a "clearing-way" for people to recall "the best of the old days that were often very tough for survival, so they become sacred," as an elder described it.

Today we often think of giving something away for our tax write-off or when someone has a house burn down. Traditionally, "giveaway" was also an activity at certain ceremonies to restore harmony and balance in the tribe by gifting others, as well as trading skills and services as a form of reciprocity or a mutual exchange of things in the tribe. In Full Circle we remind participants of gifting and giveaway in the traditional teachings. Other activities become helpers to us in being better people, or to become helpers to others, including our environment. Sometimes these activities in Full Circle can have a profound effect on people who have gotten so caught up in protecting their turf and things of value. The value of giving and awareness of the self becomes powerful lessons for all in the circle for healing.

NAMING

In the traditional American Indian way infants are given names by their parents, other family members, or even the medicine person, usually within four to seven days following birth. Names were subject to change throughout a person's lifetime according to life experiences and tribal customs. Oftentimes a name might be acquired in later life because it described something about the person or something the person had done, such as He-Leaves-His-Enemy-Lying-Face-Down-in-the-Water, or Rides-in-the-Door for a Johnny-on-the-spot kind of person.

For the Pawnee, a baby was named after birth based on his or her physical appearance or some distinguishing behavior; examples included Round Eyes, Fatty, and Young Bull. Later in life, a person received another name following marriage. A son might receive yet a third name from his father as a way of commemorating a courageous act.

In the Crow tradition of naming, a noted warrior was requested by the father to name the child according to some personal achievement on the part of that warrior. As Wendell Oswalt conveys in his book *This Land Was Theirs: A Study of North American Indians*, a woman might be named Captures-the-Medicine-Pipe, while a man might be called His-Coups-are-Dangerous. In return for this service, the warrior usually received a horse as an expression of gratitude. Though women rarely changed their names in later life, men often received a new name marking some brave deed or as a way of insuring good fortune. However, nicknames based on some unusual event or behavior were more commonly used.

According to Oswalt, a Tlingit baby was named after a maternal ancestor based on some animal associated with the clan. Later in life, a person's name might be changed if a community-wide celebration, the "potlatch," was held.

Thus, as we can see, a name received at birth may be replaced in later life due to some behavior or some outstanding act or experience by that person. In addition, names sometimes emerged following a vision or dream. As John G. Neihardt recounts, the great Sioux warrior, Crazy Horse, received his name following a powerful vision in which he witnessed a warrior atop an elaborately decorated warhorse ride wildly into battle, emerging unharmed by bullets or arrows. The horse is a sacred symbol of power; thus, this name served Crazy Horse well as he rode into one battle after another, always emerging unscathed. Naming ceremonies are still used today by some tribes, especially for babies and young people in special ceremonies. For an example of how names influence the worth of ourselves and others, view the Renaming exercise in part 3 (p. 173).

TRADITIONAL USE OF MASKS

Masks pervade virtually every society and culture of people known to humankind. For Native Americans, the mask served a very important function through its ceremonial use. Traditionally, mask wearers represented some supernatural being or sought to enlist the help of the supernatural by disguising themselves and participating in sacred rituals.

One intriguing use of masks can be found in Oswalt's account of the Iroquois. This tribe employed the mask for rituals in what is known as the False Face Society, whose duties included curing illness and keeping evil spirits at bay. Individuals became members of the False Face Society upon dreaming that they were to do so. As members of a secret society, rituals were conducted while wearing masks that represented the spiritual agents whose responsibility it was to counteract the Evil Spirit. The leader of the False Faces was said to be the Great World-Rim Dweller who, closely associated with wild animals, controlled hunters' access to wild game based upon whether or not the proper hunting taboos were observed; apologies were made to the spirits of slain animals, and there was killing only out of need. For the Iroquois, there was an integral association between wild animals and disease that was mediated by the Great World-Rim Dweller who had the ability to both cure illness and cause it. The performance of the False Faces led to the curing of illness and an eventual setting right of that which had been wronged.

The Cherokee made use of masks in what is known as the Booger Dance, usually performed in the late fall or winter. In this, a group of unidentified mask wearers disguised as "Boogers" entered domestic dwellings amid a sequence of social and animal dances and ceremony. The mask wearers, or Boogers, represented hideous ghosts or spirits that were thought to be responsible for illness or misfortune. The Boogers would dance in a circle, frightening children, making lewd gestures, and joking with adults to whom they secretly disclosed their identities. It is thought that the Booger Dance, as a symbolic ceremony, was a communal effort, through parody, to expel the disharmony introduced by disease or misfortune.

The mask, then, played an important part in allowing certain persons to perform rituals or ceremonies necessary for the harmonious functioning of the community or tribe as a whole. The mask was further used by the Cherokee to emphasize the transitory nature of various social roles that people play; the exchange of masks was used to signify a switching of roles and was deemed appropriate for certain situations and not for others. Following ceremonial participation, mask wearers often revealed their "true selves" by taking away the mask. As the Mask exercise in part 3 (p. 172) demonstrates, this exercise in self-awareness provides a helpful means for individuals to understand how they are perceived by themselves and others.

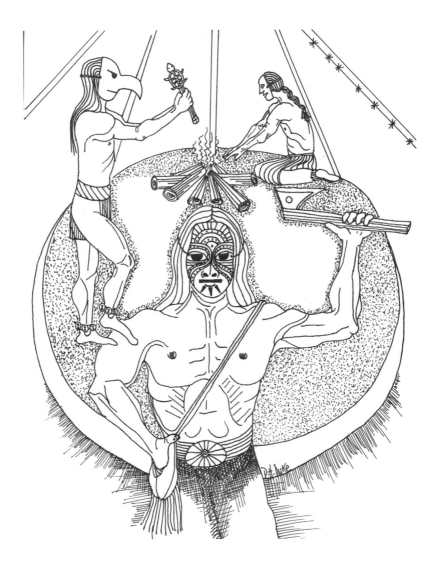

Booger Dance. Removal of the mask following the Booger Dance helps the wearer to accept him- or herself, feel clear of outside influences, and accept the way of right relationship.

RECIPROCITY AND GIVEAWAY

Ceremonies were usually held during critical times of an individual's life or to emphasize events important to the community or tribe. Ordinarily including feasting, dancing, songs, and gifts, ceremonies marked such important events as birth and death, successful battles or raids, the completion of a new house, property redistribution, or the settlement of disputes. A core value for Native Americans of all tribal origins is that of harmony and balance. Ceremonies were one way of celebrating or restoring balance within a tribe or community.

For the Tlingit, the value of balance was built into both the social and economic structures. Various interdependent segments of the society were linked through a practice involving the redistribution of goods among the people. The exchanging of gifts played an important role in the lives of everyone. In addition, it reinforced the idea of balance. Whenever a service was needed by someone who provided that service exclusively, gifts were given through an intermediary carrying the request.

Exchanges were not expected to equalize immediately, though in time, gifts should balance one another. Exchanges took various forms including barter, gift exchange, food gifts, feasts, ceremonial exchange of labor, or the potlatch (a ceremonial exchange of gifts). Indeed, social status among the Tlingit could most readily be achieved by holding a great potlatch. For this event, the host held an enormous celebration during which feasting, dancing, songs, and the distribution of gifts to members of the community took place. Essentially, the host would give away most of his possessions to those in attendance. Potlatches were rather competitive in that there was a constant effort to give an even greater potlatch than the

previous one. Oswalt relates the following account of a potlatch held to celebrate the completion of a new house in which
many community members contributed:

"As the property was being brought out, guests were paid
to dance and sing. It required four days to give out all the blankets. The house builder wore a hat that had been used by his
uncles and grandmothers; by wearing it, along with distribut-
ing so much property, he established his social position as the
Raven chief at Klukwan. The two hosts distributed about
$11,000 worth of property."

Such reciprocity demonstrated respect for others in the
community and for their willingness to give of themselves—in
this case, helping in the construction of a man's house. By
holding a potlatch, the host heightened his social standing by
restoring the balance; the one who is the most generous and
considerate is the one who is most respected. Hence, this practice ensured that the balance of goods remained constant
within the community. The potlatch is an excellent example
of a Giveaway Ceremony, in which something, usually possessions, is willingly given up or distributed to others as a way of
celebrating harmony and balance and reaffirming one's inner
strength and wisdom. Borrowing from this tradition, the Giveaway exercise in part 3 (p. 181) encourages participants to release anger and negative emotions as a means of attaining internal balance.

CONTRARY SOCIETY

Tribal societies or "clubs" often served some social or religious
function among the people. These societies were organized
and strictly regulated with a specific function to be carried
out. Sometimes smaller societies were created by those who,

for whatever reason, did not qualify for the larger, more established societies.

Among the Pawnee, the Contrary Society, sometimes referred to as the Crazy Dogs, was a smaller society created following a vision by the leaders. Organized around specific rituals, the members painted themselves black indicating that they were always ready to fight, and reversed normal expectations for behavior. The Crazy Dogs emphasized a very important lesson, the lesson of opposites, for all to witness. Moreover, they achieved considerable prestige for their bravery, and for remaining true to their cause, though their numbers dwindled to the point of disbanding after a battle in which most of the members were killed. The other warriors probably called for a retreat. The Crazy Dog technique in part 3 (p. 167) allows participants to apply the Rule of Opposites in order to disengage from habitual patterns of thinking and behaving.

SWEAT LODGE CEREMONY

In order to ensure harmony it was necessary to participate in the ritualized cleansing of the mind, body, and spirit provided for by the Sweat Lodge Ceremony. Traditionally this was a time for purifying oneself by joining with the powers of Mother Earth, and those of the Universal Circle, for giving thanks and for asking that oneself and others be blessed. Through sweating the body naturally cleanses itself of impurities, such as toxins in the blood, and also stabilizes or balances body temperature in order to survive demanding conditions. In a similar manner, the Sweat Lodge Ceremony uses this natural process to purify not only the body, but also the mind and the heart or spirit. It provides a time for "collecting" oneself, so to speak, and for healing.

Traditionally, the Sweat Lodge Ceremony was conducted on many different occasions: in preparation for the hunt; as a form of schooling for the young who would be taught their culture and myths; physical doctoring or spiritual training; or in celebration at the time of the new moon. First, a sacred place in which to conduct the ceremony would be sought, usually in close proximity to a creek, river, pond, or lake. Careful attention would be given to methods emphasizing the law of reciprocity in which something is given for everything that is respectfully taken. In his work *The Sweat Lodge: An Ancient Medicine for Modern Sicknesses,* Robert Lake elaborates on the Native American belief that "each piece, part, or element contributes a special life force and spirit to the ceremony, that all things are alive and possess a spirit, and everything in nature is a form of medicine if one knows how to recognize and use it. Each rock, for example, has its own form of communication and vibratory level which affects its energy pattern and frequency; hence it is alive. The same can be said for the trees which are not just dead wood but 'energy forces' combined with the rocks and natural elements to create a special kind of physical and spiritual energy."

The sweat lodge itself, usually a small turtle-shaped dwelling, would be constructed by searching out and asking permission from the various materials of Mother Earth (tree saplings, wood, bark, rocks) for their participation in the ceremony. The rock pit was formed in the center of the designated sacred spot around which the lodge was constructed from materials placed in relation to the four cardinal directions—east, south, west, and north—and covered with animal hides, blankets, woven mats, or bark and sod.

Meanwhile, the Fire Keeper, usually a young person, had

the responsibility of tending the sacred fire in which the ceremonial rocks were being heated. Participants in the ceremony stripped themselves of clothing and any personal belongings, such as jewelry, and entered the sweat lodge or "womb of Mother Earth" one by one, usually on their hands and knees or bowing in order to show humbleness. Next, the rocks were brought into the lodge, arranged to represent the Four Directions, and the flap or door opening was sealed shut. The darkness represented the darkness of the spirit, our ignorance, which required purification in order to have light.

After making an invocation to the Great Spirit, Mother Earth, the Four Directions, the spirits, and all the relations in nature, special water or an herbal mixture was poured over the heated rocks producing a purifying steam that filled the lodge. Participants prayed for their families, friends, each other, and themselves, asking for strength, healing, protection, blessing, or forgiveness for any harm committed against any living creature in Nature. In addition, songs might be sung, rites and rituals performed, or problems discussed. The sweat lodge functioned as a counseling center and place for group therapy. This sacred healing space allowed individuals to gather and work through marriage and family problems, personal problems, inter-family conflicts, and problems involving fears, anxieties, and depressions in a group way. Following the completion of the ceremony, participants emerged from the sweat lodge to bathe in the cooling waters of the nearby creek, river, pond, or lake. Afterward, the participants took time to reflect with one another on their experience.

All plans for the Sweat Lodge ceremony are as sacred today as the formality of church in planning what to do to prepare, such as fasting; when and how to enter the lodge; and the chants to be used to keep everything clear of unwanted spirits while a person or persons are in the sweat lodge. In some tribes only certain persons are chosen to run the sweat lodges at certain times of the month and year based on ceremony and tradition. It is important to respect those traditions and to follow the requirements for entering and exiting a sweat lodge. Everything has a purpose, based on tradition, such as the rocks used to hold the heat and the wood to make the fire to heat the rocks. There are certain plants used in "sipping fluids," and the water that is put on the rocks for steam is considered sacred. The fasting is critical, as is the temperature inside the lodge itself. These are the kind of details that can be simulated in modern society, but it is just not the same for those who have grown up with traditional sweats.

Though techniques for the Sweat Lodge Ceremony varied from tribe to tribe, the ceremony served an important function for all who participated in it through purification and healing. From the skin, bodily toxins and negative energy were released. Similarly, from the mind and spirit, toxins such as anger, frustration, hurt, or anxiety were released. Ways of dealing with various situations, with others, and with oneself were talked about within the framework of the Universal Circle represented by the sweat lodge and its sacred ceremony. While we do not undertake the sweat lodge ceremony in Full Circle gatherings, we do simulate certain activities of the sweat that emphasize the teaching and healing underlying the ceremony. The group healing process featured in part 3 of this book is modeled after the Sweat Lodge Ceremony, which acts as an excellent metaphor to the traditional emphasis of the Full Circle approach.

Full Circle ways help us to make transitions in our lives.

In the traditional teachings this is often called "crossover." An elder said, "Cross over the bridge in your mind or just walk across one of the log bridges across a creek. Allow yourself to feel the movement of leaving something behind, knowing that you return always by going into a circle. You do that even if you turn around and go back the same way you came. This time, allow yourself to feel a new or renewed understanding about making the crossover without turning around, but going forward in a positive place of healing. If you think it, so it is, regardless of the negativity or whatever else is going on around you." The next section of the book moves us into this "Healing-way."

PART TWO
Wellness and the Healing-Way

3

Being and Doing

A human being's toughest job is simply to be.
—Raccoon (Michael Tlanusta Garrett)

It was a beautifully warm day. Grandfather Sun poured his golden warmth graciously down upon the land for all of Mother Earth's creatures to enjoy. The air was crisp with a slight wind that seemed to breathe life into everything. Raccoon noticed all of this beauty very well as he went from flower to flower, leaf to leaf, rock to rock, and back to the flowers again, exploring all of Mother Earth's vast wealth. Even the most cleverly concealed hiding places were unsafe from Raccoon's probing little black and white snout. The discovery of tasty morsels such as wild blackberries occasionally halted the journey, but only long enough to chew.

And so Raccoon slowly made his way down the path to the river's edge, singing an ancient chant taught to him by his grandmother a long time ago:

> *Like the sun and the breeze, the earth and the trees,*
> *A raccoon's toughest job is simply to be;*
> *Like the rain and the sky and the way the birds fly,*
> *A raccoon's toughest job is simply to be.*

Raccoon was busily licking excess dew from the long-bladed grass when a bright orange butterfly wisped gracefully past his nose. Quick as an arrow Raccoon shot up after her, bursting with excitement, "I'll bet I can catch you, little butterfly!" The little butterfly said nothing in return but kept flitting along the way butterflies do. Meanwhile, Raccoon became temporarily distracted by the invitation to wrestle with a hollow log. Raccoon somersaulted two or three times, kicking up a cloud of dust, before resuming his pursuit. Just as he was about to catch up with the little orange butterfly, Raccoon leaped high into the air and landed tail first into the cold swirling waters of the river.

"Help me! Help me! I cannot swim!" cried Raccoon, kicking wildly about in the shallow waters. Beaver, who was nearby, ignored Raccoon, knowing full well that raccoons can swim. Just then Raccoon bumped up against one of the lower logs of a meager-looking dam that impeded the river's flow. Raccoon opened his eyes once again and stopped kicking around in the water. There, on the far side of the dam, he could see that Beaver was still hard at work, just as he had been for the passing of several moons. The little orange butterfly was nowhere to be found.

"Beaver," called out Raccoon, "your very majestic lodge has saved me from drowning in these waters and I am grateful to you." Beaver nodded in response, continuing his work of carefully and skillfully positioning the many pieces of wood in just the right way.

"Beaver," Raccoon called out once again, "we must celebrate, for this is a great occasion deserving of some honey." Raccoon dragged his soaking, scrawny hide up onto the dam near the place where Beaver was working without hesitation. Then Raccoon began shaking his whole body furiously, getting Beaver all wet with the spray of water flying every which way.

"I know of a place," Raccoon continued, "where a very plump beehive hangs from a tree limb in waiting. I'll bet it is lonely, and we should probably visit with it for a while. Not even Bear knows of this ripe place. All you would have to do, brother, is chew the tree down, and we could enjoy an afternoon snack to commemorate this occasion! Just think of that poor, round beehive, hanging there all by its self. Nearby, there is even a meadow covered with wildflowers of all colors where we can dance when we're finished."

Beaver continued laying logs and packing mud firmly into the empty crevices of his structure, saying, "I do not have time to talk with you now, Raccoon. You can see that I have work I must do." Just beneath the sound of afternoon crickets, birdsongs, and the occasional rustling of leaves, the river's water gurgled slowly, evenly.

"Beaver, many moons have come and gone," pleaded Raccoon, "and none of them have seen you playing in the long grass as I do, or watching Grandfather Sun drop below the horizon."

"Winter is coming soon," replied Beaver, working tirelessly, "and you, Raccoon, will have no secure place to live."

Looking a bit perplexed as he watched Beaver laboring, Raccoon scrunched up his little black and white snout. "But Mother Earth always provides me with a place to live as long as I thank her by appreciating all that she has to offer us."

Just as we were all once children, there is at least a little bit of Raccoon in all of us. Adults are, however, renowned for the "busy beaver" phenomena in which simply being is not enough. As adults we learn of all the responsibilities required for us to live in the "real world." Hence, we seek to develop a "true purpose" in life, setting aside the carefree smile and wonder that Raccoon has for the world in order to construct our personal dams of purpose which, oddly enough, never seem to be finished. Some of us may have even learned somewhere along the way that we are only as worthwhile as the things we accomplish. The larger the dam, the more worthwhile the person; the more "honest" work that has been done, the greater the reward, be it security, status, power, wealth, love, or anything else. Still, one simple truth remains: *We are not human doings, we are human beings.*

There is an implicit danger in sacrificing one's being for the sake of doing. Integrity and courage are such fragile commodities, and virtually priceless ones in a world that demands so much of us. Sometimes doing gives us a reason to avoid being, to avoid our own inner experience. After all, a human being's toughest job is simply to be, as Raccoon might remind us. That is not to say that doing is not okay. It is just as okay. Our challenge is to decide what is best for us, and where we can strike a balance between the two by relating what we *do* to our inner experience and vice versa.

How often do we hear people saying, "I wish I had the time . . ." and yet they do not make the time? They do not take the time to honor the relationship between being and doing, and to actively learn from it. Unfortunately, assuming that being and doing are one in the same often proves faulty. Focusing on one to the detriment of the other can lead to disharmony and feelings of emptiness.

How often do strangers, upon meeting, inquire as to the

nature of one another's occupations or means of accomplishment as an indicator of status and relative worth? Knowing what someone does for a living helps us to gauge what kind of person someone is. Upon meeting Raccoon many would describe him as lazy and rather irresponsible, we who stake the very value of our life on this earth in doing. And what happens when we run out of things to do? Well, this rarely happens. But when it does? We just find more "things" to do! It's like drilling a hole in water—only, in this case, the value of our existence depends upon whether or not we succeed in doing so.

Doing provides us with opportunities for learning. Hence the old adage: "If at first you don't succeed, try, try again." One gets the sense that it's really okay to "beat your head against the wall" as long as you are doing something. There is a very important reason for doing. Having things to do certainly adds purpose and direction to our lives; yet having things to do can also take it away.

The fundamental difference between being and doing is what sets Native American culture and mainstream American culture apart from one another. Being says, "It's enough just to be; our purpose in life is to develop the inner self." Doing meanwhile advocates applying hard work and achieving something special.

The American ideal of rugged individualism prescribes that life is similar to a ladder in which each rung should be seen as a progressive step toward increased separation or "separateness." Herein lies the true nature and reward of accomplishment. The toddler who learns to walk early is regarded as being more competent and independent and having "a bright future." This is but one of a series of "steps" that people take toward "individuality"—a gradual progression toward separateness takes place as we progress through several institutional rites of passage, including getting a driver's license, coming of age to vote, graduating from high school, going off to college, coming of age to consume alcohol, getting a job, marrying, or retiring. In order to "be our own person" it is necessary that we "find ourselves" (as though it were something we had lost) by defining our identity as a separate and distinct entity from that of "the crowd." Needless to say, accomplishment is the means through which this is achieved. Ironically, this constant struggle for separateness and distinction leads to feelings of disconnectedness in many cases. Doing may or may not provide safe haven in such instances.

For mainstream society, individual worth is measured according to one's accomplishments in life or one's potential and ambition for accomplishment. The more a person does, the more worthy that person is of respect and admiration. Since "nothing can stand in the way of progress," "the movers and shakers" are "in the fast lane" "on their way to bigger and better things."

Ironically, this societal reverence for accomplishment is not of a cumulative nature, as evidenced by the general devaluing of elders. Once people have grown older and spent their potential, their limited ability to "build dams" suddenly detracts from their intrinsic worth. After all, what are they good for then? It becomes blatantly obvious that the emphasis falls more on the doing than on the inner substance of the person. The absence of doing usually implies some form of personal inadequacy, as seen with the mainstream views and treatment of elders.

So-called inactivity is abhorred in this society, which remarks, "If you don't know what to do, at least do something!"

This is the same mainstream culture that worships "time" as a resource to be used for the sake of action. Time is a concept that was spawned by the same mind-set that developed the signature scientific approach to Western civilization. It's likely that the concept of time was originally intended to help us in guiding our lives. Strangely enough, time has become something tangible to us and has now taken on a life of its own. Reminiscent of Frankenstein brought to life, time has achieved the ability to control our lives at every level. Our preoccupation with time is well captured by Larry Brendtro, Martin Brokenleg, and Steve Van Bockern in their book *Reclaiming Youth at Risk: Our Hope for the Future*: "We make time, take time, save time, spend time, waste time, borrow time, budget time, invest time, and manage time among other things." Always, at the heart of it all, we are using time to *do* things. However, when there is nothing more to do, time becomes a burden— we find ourselves "killing" time.

It is not hard to understand why many Indian people remain confused by and mistrustful of mainstream culture and its intentions. Coupled with centuries of broken treaties and exploitation, Indian culture has seen doing for what it is in many cases—a means to an end. Mainstream culture has consistently presented Indian people with two choices: "Be (do) like us, or don't be." After all, what kind of existence can there be without the progress achieved in doing?

The Indian way of life emphasizes being over doing. While mainstream culture asks, "What do you do for a living?" as a quick indicator of who someone is and what that person's relative worth might be, Indian culture asks, "Where do you come from, who's your family?" Being derives much of its power from connectedness. One of the most important sources of connection is the family. "If you know my family, then you know me."

Being is a difficult state to maintain without a strong sense of belonging to serve as a foundation. An Indian person meeting someone for the first time already assumes that person to be worthy of respect as a fellow member of the Universal Circle. The remaining issue to be established is, "What is the strength of his or her sense of belonging?" As Wynne DuBray observes in her article "American Indian Values: Critical Factor in Casework," "About the most unfavorable moral judgment an Indian can pass on another person is to say 'he acts as if he didn't have any relatives.'"

For an Indian person, belonging and connectedness lie at the very heart of one's self-identity. These values provide important answers to questions such as, "Where do I come from?" "Who am I?" and "Where do I belong?" Several studies have indicated the Indian preference for being. As Wynne DuBray points out, Indians tend "to choose being over doing, which implie[s] that intrinsic worth is more important than education, status, power, or wealth." But what is intrinsic worth? Is there such a thing?

As discussed earlier, Native American spirituality is deeply rooted in the Principle of Noninterference, which focuses on the harmony created by the connection with all parts of the universe. All things have a purpose and value exemplary of "personhood," including plants ("tree people"), animals ("our four-legged brothers and sisters"), rocks and minerals ("rock people"), the land ("Mother Earth"), the winds ("the Four Powers"), "Father Sky," "Grandfather Sun," "Grandmother Moon," and so on. Within this view lies the truest sense of belonging. Being essentially requires only that we seek our place in the

universe; everything else will follow. Since everyone and everything was created with a specific purpose to fulfill, we do not
have the power to interfere or to impose upon others our views
of the best path to follow.

So who is right, we may ask, the Beaver or the Raccoon?
Maybe they are both right. It is really no one's place to say
whether we should slave away building dams or run around
frolicking like raccoons. However, each of us in our search for
whatever it is that we seek has the ability to temper one against
the other, Beaver and Raccoon, doing and being. And what is
the lesson of being? That is for you to decide.

In my (J. T.'s) book *Meditations with the Cherokee,* there are
many meditations and activities to celebrate just "being." There
is one that can definitely put us in touch with all the elements
and energy of our own being. First, find a time when time
does not matter, which can probably be just about any time
you choose. Second, find a place that really matters to you,
such as a special spot, a tree, a rock, a place at the ocean, or
just lying down on the ground so you are in touch with Mother
Earth and can feel the calmness of Father Sky. Make sure you
will not be startled or interrupted for a few minutes by your
cell phone or by others who do not respect your space. Animals will leave you alone because they can sense your sacred
space, except for the little insects that consider you in the way,
and they enjoy your heat. Of course, a little puppy or dog will
find this a time to play because they seek so much attention.
Allow yourself the chance to just float by feeling yourself move
within the energy flow around you.

Allow yourself at least four minutes to just simply float,
knowing that you are connected to Mother Earth and that
she will protect you. Say the chant "ou no lea he" four times

slowly, then allow yourself to simply "be." Feel the flow of energy in nature and breathe deeply using the belly, rather than the chest. In a circle with friends it can be magical! Alone or with friends in a circle you can enjoy relaxing, feeling the flow of energy in your own body, as well as the sensation of energy and life of the Universal Circle that surrounds you. With some practice you can do this in a boring meeting with your eyes open, while your conscious mind takes in and responds to whoever thinks they are saying something important for you to hear. The point is that you are truly connected to the energy of the Universal Circle of life around you. You can learn being and doing at the same time, while relaxing and healing. It is also a good way to receive messages and enjoy time well spent with yourself.

4
Underlying Assumptions

I think it is time you knew of Tagoona, the Eskimo. Last
year one of our white men said to him, "We are glad you
have been ordained as the first priest of your people. Now
you can help us with their problem."

Tagoona asked, "What is a problem?"

And the white man said, "Tagoona, if I held you by your heels
from a third-story window, you would have a problem."

Tagoona considered this long and carefully. Then he said, "I
do not think so. If you saved me, all would be well. If you
dropped me, nothing would matter. It is you who
would have the problem."

—MARGARET CRAVEN,
I Heard the Owl Call My Name

There are several basic truths governing both the intent and
process involved with Full Circle healing and wellness. The
assumptions we hold about life influence the way we live. An
implicit wisdom is assumed to dwell within all of us only to
be unlocked through experience. Whether or not we listen to
it, however, is thought to simply be a question of personal
choice. This too is a part of experience. *We may not always have*

control over what happens to us, but we always have a choice over what happens inside us.

Our choices carry consequences and implications wherein lies the potential for learning. The following are but a few simple truths underlying the idea of moving Full Circle: The following are a few simple truths based on traditional American Indian beliefs to help you to understand the values underlying the Full Circle.

There are times in life when the son becomes the teacher and the father listens. This section is one of those times. Michael listened with reverence to me, as the father, espouse the wisdom of our ancestors; he also listened intently as participants in Full Circle gatherings asked many questions about their own limitations in seeking guidance. From his listening Michael created these statements in the Full Circle teachings to help us better understand that our ancestors are not something in the past, but they are here with us in every thought and in every cell of our bodies. More importantly, we have the wonderful gifts of choice and critical thinking. The turtle when born knows to go toward the light of the moon to return to the ocean. Our responsibility is to not put up man-made lights that confuse the turtles, which can result in their deaths rather than life. Michael's statements summarize much thinking and discussions in Full Circle about personal choice and ownership of thoughts and actions.

> **We are our own best experts.** No one knows us better than us. Nobody but us has seen with our eyes the things we've seen, and most importantly, no one but us has experienced our lives in quite the same way that we have. What others do know of us, they know only

through what they see and what we tell them. It is our choice whether or not to invite others to see with our eyes or walk in our shoes; it is their choice whether or not to do so.

We are our own worst enemies. No one does a better job of deceiving us or treating ourselves badly than we do. No one can do a better job of finding ways to ignore our innermost thoughts and fears than we can. Certainly, other people may try to make us feel badly, or want us to be different than we are; however, their success depends on our willingness to let them succeed in doing so. Our success in doing ourselves wrong depends solely on intention.

You don't always have to talk to say what you mean. The things that we do and say are never as important as the way in which we do or say them. Likewise, people tend to listen more to *what they see* than *what they hear*. Words are merely tools for the expression of what cannot otherwise be easily understood. Listening with your eyes is a skill that takes much time and willingness. We all have as much right to express ourselves with silence as we do with words. Neither words nor silence are more important than the respect one person holds for another in the realization of the humanity shared by both.

Words are just words. We most often think of communication in terms of the words we speak; it could even be argued that we think in words. Clearly, words are important to us, but words are nothing more than "tools." We use them for our purposes and they are used with us and upon us. However, words have no absolute meaning outside of context and we should not assume that they do. We give words power and can also take that power away. We accept certain things as being true and, in turn, create truths for ourselves; words help us do this and they are only as real as we make them. Since so much of living involves interacting with others, we must be aware of the meanings and intentions that words may or may not convey in an effective way. At the same time, we have to restrain ourselves from "reading too much into things." Words say a lot about us and the things around us, but *words are not us.*

Nothing is good or bad until we decide that it is. All of the things around us are, in themselves, neither good nor bad. Judgments of good and bad are purely subjective, though it is sometimes easy to forget that true worth is independent of thinking. By the same token, the power of assigning a perceived sense of worth applies to oneself. Thus, within a given set of circumstances we can make and remake ourselves upon choosing, just as we perceive one thing as good and another as bad.

The worst thing about having so many choices is having to choose. No one can say for sure who is truly worse off: the one who is forced to do something and wishes she or he could do something entirely different, or the one who freely chooses to do something and later regrets it.

Imagination is the one true measure of freedom. It's not a matter of what you can or cannot do, but what you *think* you can or cannot do that matters. Inevitably, the rest will follow in time. Being open to experience or the possibilities of every situation reflects the inner strength of one who has established harmony within oneself.

It's possible to have an answer before you've thought of the question. How much easier would life be if we gave ourselves the credit we truly deserve? Luckily, some of us have that one person in our lives who believes we have the answer inside of ourselves and encourages us to listen. Indeed, the most trusted friend we will ever know lives in our own skin.

Wisdom is having more questions than answers. The one who has found all the answers to his or her questions has run out of questions. The one who has run out of questions has run out of learning. A person who ceases to learn has also ceased to experience. And a person who has run out of experience cannot be wise.

Search long and hard enough for something and you'll surely find it. Sometimes we look for something where there is nothing. However, if we keep looking for it to be there, almost miraculously it will be—this is especially true of limitations. Moreover, the harder we look for a certain quality or limitation, the more likely it is to appear before our very eyes. At the same time, if you look too hard for something you might miss it altogether.

Sometimes we try so hard to be what we're not that we forget who we are. Our nature provides us with opportunities for becoming something much greater than ourselves. However, if a circle tries to bend by ignoring its center, it's no longer a circle.

You cannot lose what you never had to begin with. It may only seem natural for us to want to assume control over those things where we have none. Strangely, we are talented at fooling ourselves when we so choose. Feelings of regret often lead to guilt, anger, or doubt. Ownership over anything, other than that which makes us human, can make life more difficult than it has to be.

Forever is now. To dwell on the past means to forfeit the present; to dwell on the future means to forget where you are and from where you have come. Re-creation of the past and speculation about the future serves an important purpose. Sometimes we look for a point of reference in our lives; sometimes we need to escape the demands of living. But sometimes we need to just cherish the moment—even a painful one—by appreciating where we are and gathering strength from the knowledge that there will never be another one exactly like it. Meanwhile, that moment is rapidly becoming our past and fulfilling our future. Ultimately, that moment in time is part of a greater experience that has a deeper meaning for us than the passing pain or pressures of daily living.

5

The Sacred Tree of Life

The Sacred Tree of Life, with its roots firmly planted, its trunk strong but flexible, and its branches and leaves calling out to the four winds reminds us of our place in the world. In many Native American traditions, to "offer prayers" means calling out to the four winds for the spirit of each direction from which that wind comes to bring its sacred power to us as we continue our journey of life. As we look to each of the winds for harmony and balance we must consider the sacred lessons offered to us by each of the four directions, and by the Universal Circle itself. The Universal Circle is included in every aspect of the Native American way of life. It starts with the creation of harmony and balance symbolized by the Sacred Tree of Life.

One of the purposes in living is growing. When a small acorn falls to the ground and eventually becomes embedded in the warm heart of Mother Earth, there is opportunity for growth. With the showering of sunshine and rain, the acorn gathers strength from the Earth as it begins spreading its roots deeper into the dirt and sprouting its stem toward daylight. With the passing of time and the nurturance of Mother Earth, Father Sun, and the rain, the acorn grows from a small seedling into a little sapling, its arms outstretched, moving ever-slowly toward the sky. The young tree, constantly reaching upward and outward from its core, grows into an older tree, taking nutrients from its surrounding while simultaneously giving of its life, fruits, and protective shade in a delicate balance of nature. The tree strives to grow strong, facing adversity in storms, lightning, and drought to become what it is and always seeking to become what it can be, even in the face of hardship.

It is said that the Creator planted a Sacred Tree for all the people of Earth. There, they would find healing, power, wisdom, and security. The tree would be firmly grounded, its roots reaching deeply into the body of Mother Earth, its trunk and branches spread up and outward, giving thanks for all life. The fruits borne would be the sacred teachings showing the path to love, compassion, wisdom, justice, courage, respect, and modesty. It is thought that the life of the One Tree is the life of the people. We are all like the Sacred Tree. We live and experience the changing of the seasons, the changing of our lives. We weather the storms couragously, though we sometimes feel stripped bare of our protective foliage, the earth turned up and eroding at our very feet. And yet, given the opportunity to give ourselves the choice, we renew ourselves. We grow both in sunshine and in rain.

We experience a sense of belonging and connectedness with other trees, the forest, other creatures, the sky, the earth. We feel a sense of mastery at producing whatever fruits we are most capable of and revel in our successful endurance of the conditions. We experience a sense of independence at being a tree unique from other kinds of trees, unique from the other creatures, unique unto ourselves insofar as no other tree has experienced exactly the same things nor in the same way. We are filled with a sense of generosity through an openness to

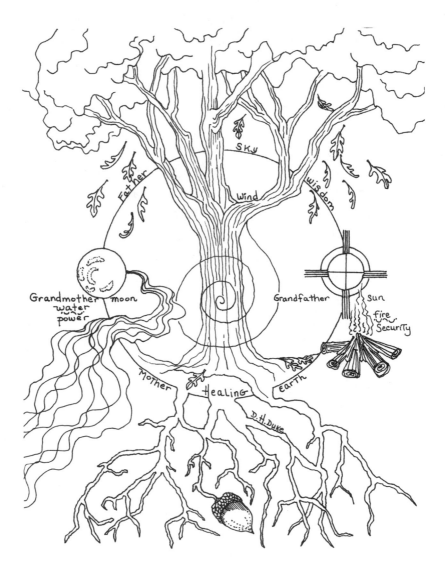

The tree embodies the sacred connection of all things
in the Universal Circle of life.

experience, and genuine ability to give of our shelter, shade, fruit, leaves, bark, branches, oxygen—to give of ourselves so that other creatures may also live, and that together we may live in harmony. Experiencing all of these things leads us to a gradual expansion and strengthening of layer upon layer built on courage and wisdom; this is the very pith of our being. We are many-colored with different sizes, shapes, and ages. Still, at the heart of it all, and at the core of our experiences, we are all trees.

Sometimes, as mentioned, the storms strip us of our beautiful leaves or the droughts drain us of our physical strength. Or sometimes, in all our splendor, we neglect our trunks, extending our branches too far or too high or simply growing too many branches to where the slightest shift in breeze may throw us out of balance—our once firmly planted selves left to sway loosely in midair. We may place too much on our branches or allow others to load our branches to the point of breaking. Then we sway heavily one way or the other away from our center of gravity. We may cower at the thought that our roots are too few or too shallow and forget to drink the earth's water and rich nutrients. We may so anticipate being struck down that the strain of worry or doubt can, in itself, split our very heartwood, leaving us in a gradual state of decay that moves from the inside out.

We may forget our connection with other trees; we may stifle the growth of our fruits; we may forget our own uniqueness and our ability to make ourselves; we may close ourselves off or fail to give of ourselves or the gifts we have to offer, or we may give away more than we have to offer. All of these things may come from fear or from devastation, and all of these things can leave us unbalanced, unable to cope, and full of disharmony.

These are times for remembering the lessons taught to us by the Sacred Tree of Life.

As an elder said, "This [Sacred Tree of Life] is one of the simplest lessons for us to learn, but it can be one of the most complex to really understand. We are connected to the tree and the tree is us, in a way. We are truly connected to the seasons, like the tree itself. We are truly connected to Mother Earth, for without her we would die for lack of food and water. It is important that we teach our children these lessons so they understand their connections." To understand the connection that elders refer to with the circle of life or the Sacred Tree of Life it is helpful to relate to the Four Directions.

In traditional teachings of American Indians the circle represents an energy that is everywhere in the universe. It starts with the formation of an original cell or circle that is in spirit. This spirit originates with the Great One, which comes to life-form in the presence of the "thunder beings," as described by earlier Cherokee. Earlier indigenous people that spent so much time in nature must have been in awe of the 50,000 thunderstorms that can occur every day on Mother Earth. The electrical power that can strike the earth, as well as meteors that can also have booms, are powerful events. These events could create sacred fire, and even the trees that were struck were considered as sacred wood used for ceremonies and healing. Earlier scientific minds envisioned this same power as being in our bodies to a lesser extent; it created life, but it had to originate from somewhere outside in the spirit world. That world was the "skyvault" where the Great One resided and looked over our Mother Earth.

The center of the circle of life was a sacred fire started by the "thunder beings" as an "apportioner" with the Sun, which also created plant life and food for every living thing to survive. Of course, everything, even the rocks, were considered as having energy, including the energy to heal. This is why we have Medicine that includes the rocks, such as crystals, and the plants with energy to heal. The trees that provide shelter and protection also provide healing when we sit or lie below the branches. As an elder said, "We are an extension of nature, and she is an extension of us. We are one with everything. We cannot breathe without the trees and plants, and they cannot live without us." The exchange goes beyond oxygen and carbon dioxide; it is about an energy that connects us to the spirit of all things. This represents the sacred fire that we call life.

This circle of life is taught as having four cardinal directions that existed long before the idea of North, South, East, and West existed. The names for these directions in the old language describe a state or being that influences us, such as North affecting our mental state; South affecting our natural state; East affecting our spiritual state; and West affecting our physical state. This is what we espouse in the Full Circle teachings as the Four Directions. It is very difficult to describe these states in words; they do not fully convey the feelings that people experience in the traditional exercises and activities. However, the positive experiences tell us that people seem to have some innate sense of connection with the Four Directions.

THE FOUR DIRECTIONS

An elder said, "The East is the direction of the rising sun, and the West is the direction of the moon. They both provide light and energy, and they both had the same name in the old language. We did not call it day and night. In the old days there was no day or night any more than there was good and bad.

These opposites were of the same energy." The direction of the East and the West represent the balance in our lives, from the spiritual in the East to the physical in the West. The East is symbolized by the Golden Eagle, while the West has the Bison or the Bear. "The old ones would say that we learn to be close families and clans in the East, but we are always aware of the protection and competition of the West. On the other hand, in the West we can get too caught up in physical strength and endurance or being a warrior to realize why we are that way in the first place. It is to be a protector of our families and clans for survival of our way of life," said the elder.

In Full Circle we have activities to learn how this balance is so important to us that we can lose our perspective, such as in competition where we get too focused on winning. On the other hand we can get so biased in our spiritual way that we forget to be humble and we try to force our beliefs on others. The balance becomes a strong connection between family and spirituality, with physical survival through hard work to provide for the family. For some people work becomes a competition and a way to win and gain more and more. They lose perspective on being a helper to the family and others. They become driven by the physical gain rather than the spiritual gain. The balance of East and West is healthy and adds positive energy to the circle.

An elder said, "The North is a place of quiet in nature, whereas the South is a place of play in nature. It is a way of harmony, rather than balance." The old stories of going to the North or the cold land is always about finding a sacred place or an enchanted land where it is warm and everything is abundant. Going to the South is a place of finding the ocean or enjoying the warm sun while playing with the small animals. The North is a place of calm and quiet, while the South is a place of music, dance, and a time to enjoy life. The traditional activities and exercises focus on finding that spot or place of harmony in our lives.

There is a Cherokee story of the North coming to visit the South and seeing the daughter of the South as a beautiful young woman, dancing and enjoying the warm sunshine. He falls in love with her and wants to take her to his home of ice in the North, which he finally does. The North land people become concerned because all the ice is melting, and they fear for their lives. After much consideration for the harmony of life for the North land people, he decides that he must take his beautiful bride back to her home in the South. She is sad because she has to return home, but she dances in the warm sun with closed eyes to dream of her love in the North. Story goes that the North every once in a while drifts down to the South to watch his beautiful bride dance in the warm sum. Sometimes she dances to the direction of the North to spend time with her love of the North. And they say that is the reason we have weather changes from the North to the South and vice versa.

The North is the direction of learning and sharing. The elders say that, for those people who become too much like a book worm, it is important that they go to the South to enjoy the warm sun, to dance and play. For those who play too much it is important to learn a skill and focus more time on learning and sharing. It is the harmony that one learns to develop or finds when needed that keeps the mental strong and alert, while enjoying nature.

CIRCLE OF LIFE

The circle of life begins with the fire in the center, the birth, that spirals into the direction of the East for the protection of family while developing. Then life spirals to the direction of the South to learn how to play, "and to learn of the fairness of games in nature." At about the age of seven we start our spiral to the direction of the West, where we learn competition and endurance for work and play through the teen years. Then we spiral to the direction of the North, where we learn the skills and knowledge of an adult to be a teacher and master of our abilities or trade. We continue to spiral until we reach our elder years as we return to the sacred fire of life, to begin again in the spirit world as ancestors.

This is the Universal Circle of life that brings us the understanding through the Sacred Tree of Life and our connections with all things within the circle.

6
The Universal Circle

The Sacred Seven is the Four Directions of North, South, West, and East with the Upper World, Lower World, and the Center as the Sacred Fire. All things exist in the Four Directions within the Universal Circle.
—As told by Tlanusta (Walkingstick)

There was a time when Sun would cross over the Little People working in their planting fields while going to the house of Grandmother in the sky vault. Sun was bothered by the Little People squinting and making faces as the people looked up into the bright sunshine. Sun decided to be even brighter to the Little People. Of course they would cover their eyes and avoid looking into the sunshine. Sun felt hurt and decided to not come out of the sky house to make the journey to visit with Grandmother. For many days it was dark. The corn stalks and beans began to turn brown, and the people said, "We must go to council and decide what is to be done, otherwise we will starve this winter with no corn and beans harvested." They met in council, and the Great Bear said, "I will go up to the sky vault and drag Sun out of the sky house with my strength." The council members thought that would just irritate Sun, and some felt it would be best to encourage cooperation with

Sun. They rejected the idea of Rattlesnake scaring Sun out of the sky house. An elder Medicine Man suggested that he knew a way to make things right with Sun. The council agreed, and he turned himself into the Great White Eagle for the long journey. He returned to tell the story of how Sun thought that all the Little People were making faces and did not like Sun.

The agreement was made to have a special ceremony to Sun with dancing and a great feast called Green Corn Ceremony. Suddenly, the Medicine Man was no longer to be seen and little else was said about the disappearance. Sun was very happy and continued to make the journey to Grandmother's house. The next planting season a large flower of bright yellow appeared, and more followed as the Little People planted corn and beans. Many suggested that the agreement made between Sun and the Medicine Man had something to do with the appearance of the flowers we call sunflowers today. Of course, others say it was just time for the Medicine Man to go on his own journey. At any rate, the Eagle Dance of the Cherokee and the Green Corn Ceremony or Fall Festival of today continues to give thanks and celebration to Sun for good corn and beans to survive the long winters.

The sun and the eagle are symbols of the East in Cherokee myths and stories. They represent the spirit of **clarity** and **honesty**. The small animals such as the beaver or the rabbit are symbols of the South that represent the spirit of **innocence** and **renewal**. The bear is a symbol of the West that represents the spirit of **introspection** and **strength**. The deer, wolf, and hawk are symbols of the North, representing the spirit of **trust** and **purity**. This is the Medicine of the Four Directions that has many varieties of animals, birds, mammals,

In the Green Corn Ceremony we celebrate the Sun's gift
in the creation of life.

The Four Directions connect us with the spirit of the animals and birds as our brothers and sisters in the Universal Circle.

and fish that are used as symbols of directions or teachings by various tribes.

Indian Medicine is a unique system of healing and beliefs that are interwoven in all aspects of the four powers or Four Directions of physical, mental, spiritual, and natural that comprise the Circle of Life. While each of us has our own Medicine, it is influenced by our environment and all things within our circle of influence. The Medicine Wheel often used in American Indian teachings represents our Medicine that is symbolized by influences in the Four Directions.

The Medicine Wheel represents the Circle of Life or the Universal Circle that is within our sphere of influence. Of course, there are things outside of our circle that we cannot influence, such as the stars, but they have an influence on us. While they may be outside of our Medicine Circle and may not be represented in our Four Directions, they are within the Universal Circle. The teachings of Full Circle held each six months by us on the Cherokee Indian Reservation and other selected locations teach these "ways" for personal growth and understanding of the wonderful traditional Indian Medicine teachings.

EAST: PATH OF THE SUN

The direction of the East embodies the **spiritual** aspect of living that is a part of both personal truths and interpersonal experiences. In traditional teachings the great eagle represents the East. The eagle feather is used in sacred ceremonies and is always treated with honor and respect. While this direction is about spirituality, the eagle also mates for life and has a commitment to its young. Early Cherokee values focused on the family as an element of tribal protection, and on the provision

Eagle teaches us strength and commitment to family
in the direction of the East.

of family needs for harmony and balance. As an elder put it, "The eagle feather is two colors, black and white, while the plume in early years is gray. It teaches the lessons about everything being in twos, such as male–female, for nature to always survive as long as the eagle flies free in the skyvault above."

East represents the power of truth that comes from knowing our place in the universe, a unity with our relations and the energy that lies at the heart of creation. Here is a sense of belonging that is fostered through caring relations among people and all living creatures.

Traditionally, it was the unspoken duty of all adults to care for children and act as teachers of wisdom and skills that most often were learned by observing. From the security of these relationships the child was able to venture forth into a world rich with experiences. Any given child was cared for by a series of significant others that extended beyond the biological parents, most often to the grandparents. However, kinship ties were viewed as exemplifying the sense of relatedness felt by all in the community or tribe.

This sense of relatedness extended beyond people to the very surroundings themselves. Children learned that they were not only a part of all people, but a part of all of creation as well. A universal sense of belonging was instilled through the belief that all plants, animals, people, and things are interrelated and should be treated with dignity and respect. Striving to maintain ecological harmony was one way of ensuring personal harmony. Human relationships were viewed in much the same way.

SOUTH: PATH OF PEACE

The direction of the South embodies the **natural** way of youthful innocence represented by curiosity, playfulness, and innovation or creativity.

The rabbit in early Cherokee stories is like the coyote of some West and Southwest tribes. He is always getting himself into trouble but he always seems to get out of things all right. Ironically, the rabbit always surprises himself that he manages to get himself free of his own bolstering and tricks. As an Elder says, "The rabbit seems to always make himself look silly or foolish, but he also teaches to know better. Once the rabbit got caught in the laurels and a passerby got him free. When home he told his mother that he tripped on a log that fell in his path by the wind. He knew that he was not supposed to be out near the laurel branches because his mother always told him it was not safe. Of course he lied to his mother. His uncle came strolling in and said, 'So how did you get out of the laurels? I saw the Medicine Man who said you were crying 'cause you could not get loose.' The rabbit always got caught in his lies and deception."

There is a story of Rabbit learning how to fish, where he tells Otter that he too is good at fishing. Of course Otter challenges him to show his skill. For some reason Rabbit does not expect to be challenged. Now he has to figure out what to do, so he ties a grass reed together to make a loop and hides his device from Otter. Rabbit jumps into the water and loops a fish, which just happens to be in the mouth of a large bird that flies high into the sky. Of course, Rabbit hangs on and goes flying into the sky with a look of surprise on his face, while Otter and others laugh at his antics.

Rabbit teaches us that we only fool ourselves with our foolishness.
The key is to learn to play fair and share our gifts with others.

This story conveys the value of telling the truth, an important lesson for children as well as adults. The rabbit teaches us to not try to trick others or to lie for our own advantage. Young people always enjoy the stories of the rabbit and his adventures. While usually playful, they always reinforce the values of telling the truth and being honest about your abilities and gifts.

The South symbolizes the growth that comes from living in harmony with nature. It is a time of learning with curiosity as one develops from a child into a young adult. In the traditional way, the goal of learning was for the person to develop competence in each of the Four Directions. This could not be achieved, however, until the lesson of self-mastery had been learned. A young person is taught that wisdom can be achieved by watching and listening to the elders. Therefore, stories and ceremonies are useful ways of experiencing cultural ideals and celebrating traditions. In addition, competence was fostered through games and creative play that stimulate the learning of respect and understanding.

WEST: PATH OF INTROSPECTION

The direction of the West embodies the **physical** aspect of living and the strength that comes from knowing ourselves well; both of these inherently affect self-awareness and perceptions of autonomy.

There is a story about Black Bear, who used to just collect honey and never would share with anyone. As the story goes, Black Bear was lonely and had no friends. One day when young Beaver was working on a dam that would be strong for the rough winter months, he saw Black Bear catching fish and throwing them back into the water. He spoke to Black Bear

Bear and Beaver become friends. Bear teaches us about strength
of our youth, gifted to help others in the direction of the West.

and asked him for help in moving some poplar and locust tree trunks so he could have a strong home. Black Bear was rude and told Beaver to go away, but Beaver pleaded about the bear's strength and he had no one to help him. Black Bear felt needed because of his strength and endurance, so he helped Beaver. As the rough flash flood and cold winter set in on the mountain, Black Bear came out of his cave before hybernation to check on Beaver, who was safe and sound because of the large tree trunks used to make Beaver's home. They are still friends today.

The lesson of the bear teaches us the power of strength and introspection. Bear lives by his own strength and knows the ways of life because he has taken the time to know his own ways. Though Bear is strong, he is also gentle and introspective about all decisions by reaching deep within his own heart for answers that are sought. The direction of West symbolizes the strength that comes to us from taking the time to master our skills of survival. As an elder said, "Sometimes we need to be a little less Bear and learn to 'bare' our feelings to have a friend."

Traditionally, Native American culture has placed great importance on self-determination and autonomy. Within the circle each of us must discover who we are, what we believe in, and what's important to us. By defining ourselves we define our surroundings through an autonomy that leads us to our own personal or inner consciousness. Therefore, independence becomes crucial to developing an inner strength required to create ourselves out of what we are given. However, traditional Native American belief simultaneously emphasizes the idea that independence requires a certain degree of dependence. In other words, in order to achieve true independence one must respect and value others and all living things. Learning is a matter of choosing and accepting at will. Our will finds its roots in the heart of what we believe to be true. Choices are made with regard to maintaining both personal harmony and respect for all of our relations.

NORTH: PATH OF QUIET

The direction of the North embodies the **mental** aspect of inner consciousness and wisdom turned outward.

Earlier Cherokee respected the deer so much that the hunters would be as much like the deer as possible, even using the movements of the deer to be quiet and aware of every sound. One of the greatest hunters was Youngdeer, who even learned to run like the deer and catch smells in the wind. Some used to say that he looked so much like a deer when he adorned himself with a deerskin that once he was mistaken for a deer and almost shot with a bow and arrow.

As an elder by the name of Youngdeer once said, "Chero kee were great hunters, not just for their skill, but because they knew the Medicine and spirit of the deer. They would always give thanks to the deer for all that the deer would mean in feeding the families of the human ones, as well as the use of the deerskin to keep warm in the winter. Prayer and gifting was always done after the taking of the deer because the hunter was also the protector of all the animals and the winged-ones. We knew our place in the Universal Circle of Life."

North symbolizes the wisdom that teaches us to become masters of our trade, like Youngdeer, and to develop understanding of nature. There is much to learn from nature that provides us much advantage today. Earlier Cherokee enjoyed many stories of the stars and the "lessons of the skyvault" as a

We learn calm and healing in the direction of the North.
We learn to be generous and sharing of our gifts
and skills to benefit all things in life.

mystery that we are always seeking to understand. Learning the skills of mastery and the mysteries of life is a gift to be shared for the "benefit of everyone in the tribe," or for all beings here on Mother Earth.

The earlier ceremonies of the North were about Giveaway or a way to gift those without any expectation. It was about honoring the tribe and its members with the abundance that is available as a result of harvest before the winter. While the cold winter months were a time for focusing on survival, the winter also has a mystery to it as well. It was a time to store food and to strengthen the family ties with sharing, which was also a gift of the North.

The true gift of consciousness is thought to rest in the human ability for generosity and unselfishness, for it is here that universal truths reveal themselves most readily. Consequently, these are among the highest virtues of Native American culture.

7
Full Circle: Vision-Way

*Grandmother Moon comes up each evening, as does
Grandfather Sun to brighten our night and day. It is a
Circle of Life that affects the tides, our moods, and even our
planting seasons. Since we are kin to all things, we are
influenced by these journeys of night and day in our Circle
of Life. Therefore, our vision and truth is influenced by the
lessons of this circle journey in the Universal Circle.
This is part of our Medicine-way.*

—Doc Amoneeta Sequoyah,
Cherokee Medicine Elder

Whenever we stop long enough to observe the simple truth stated here by Doc Amoneeta Sequoyah, it reveals itself to us quite readily. At the very heart of the Indian way of life is a worldview that emphasizes the Circle of Life, represented through the Medicine Wheel. The Circle of Life symbolizes the innumerable circles that surround us, that exist within us, and of which we are all a part.

The circle, as a sacred symbol, reminds us that what we often see as progression or growth is, indeed, cyclical in nature. The entire universe moves and works in circles. Nature progresses only so long as the many ongoing and contingent cycles that permit the process of life to continue in its extraordinary and intricately balanced fashion. We, too, move and work in circles and spirals. The Circle of Life holds this truth for us. Its components—Spirit, Nature, Body, and Mind—comprise the Four Directions represented in the Circle of Life and the Medicine Wheel. Accordingly, we grow and mature, experiencing what life offers us, learning and relearning, until often we find ourselves circling back to the simple truths of childhood; we acquire more and more wisdom, only to understand the simplicity of things that mysteriously elude us as we circle through our own life cycle. Finally we share that wisdom as wisdom was once shared with us. The Circle of Life shows us the relation we have to all living things, to life itself.

THE INNER CIRCLE

Very often we seek to know ourselves, to understand what it is that makes us move in our circles and spirals, some of which are uncomfortable. To this end, the Inner Circle, corresponding to the Circle of Life, consists of Four Dimensions—**belonging, mastery, independence,** and **generosity**—that provide a framework for understanding human nature and working within its realm. A balancing of these Four Dimensions completes the Inner Circle, which in turn creates harmony within us. Insofar as people are self-determining, personal harmony or disharmony is a choice, as is the resulting wellness or unwellness that follows from a series of decisions made throughout a lifetime.

Human beings presume that there are certain qualities that distinguish us from other living creatures. A wise woman elder once said, "We all need four things in life: someone to love, something to do, something to believe in, and something to look forward to." The Inner Circle provides us with these simple truths.

We have the need for love; a yearning to give and receive recognition and affirmation **(belonging)**. We have the need to know and accept ourselves and want to feel worthwhile unto others **(generosity)**. We desire meaning in our lives, some sense that our lives possess purpose and direction from which we choose our will **(independence)**. And it is from all of these things that we make important decisions about who we are and who we are becoming. Humanity endows us with this unique capability **(mastery)**.

The Four Dimensions allow our life decisions to be better understood in terms of the circle. Moreover, the Four Dimensions are a part of every one of us, as we each possess our own unique Inner Circle. Within the Inner Circle:

Belonging is characterized by the presence of trust and caring in relations with others: **"Where do you belong or not belong?"**

Mastery is manifested by a recognition of abilities and a person's sense of meaningful achievement in his or her life: **"What are the sources of your strengths and your limits?"**

Independence represents a belief in oneself through the presence of self-awareness and self-discipline: **"What do you believe in; what is important to you?"**

Generosity is characterized by an openness to experience, represented by the ability for trust and sharing: **"What do you have to offer and want to receive?"**

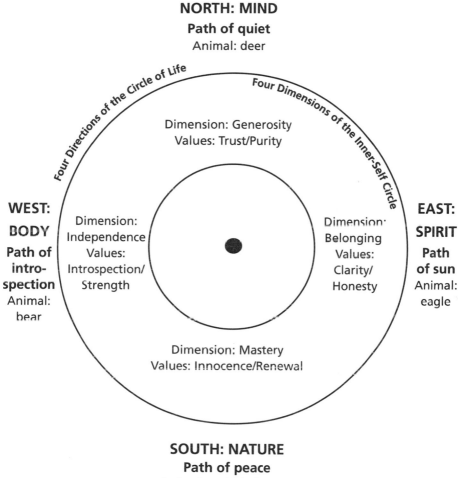

NORTH: MIND
Path of quiet
Animal: deer

Four Directions of the Circle of Life

Four Dimensions of the Inner-Self Circle

Dimension: Generosity
Values: Trust/Purity

WEST:
BODY
Path of
intro-
spection
Animal:
bear

Dimension:
Independence
Values:
Introspection/
Strength

Dimension:
Belonging
Values:
Clarity/
Honesty

EAST:
SPIRIT
Path
of sun
Animal:
eagle

Dimension: Mastery
Values: Innocence/Renewal

SOUTH: NATURE
Path of peace
Animals: rabbit, beaver

The Universal Circle and the Inner Circle

Each dimension represents a continuum along which our development in *being* proceeds. No one dimension is more important than the others; each dimension is equally important in varying levels at different points in a given lifetime. In addition, all are interrelated. For instance, the way in which we interact with our world and the views that we hold depend in part on the extent to which we experience a sense of belonging through mutual support and caring. However, it is the presence of belonging that also provides a context by which we define who we are and what is important in our lives. Hence, the dimensions are complementary.

Each of the Four Dimensions can be characterized as being present or absent in our lives. The magnitude of each dimension in our lives represents our *being*. These Four Dimensions are established and maintained through our various daily activities by the following:

1. Sharing

2. Cooperation

3. Exploration

4. Introspection

5. Definition

6. Reflection

7. Teaching

As we shall see in part 3 there are several techniques and exercises that can help us to balance ourselves as persons, to explore or reaffirm who we are, and to recognize what we are seeking. Through these explorations the presence or absence of each of the Four Dimensions in our lives becomes easier to recognize and thereby to rebalance. We begin to determine which directions are strong for us and which are weak.

CHARACTERISTICS OF THE FOUR DIMENSIONS

Dimension	Present	Absent
Belonging	Caring, Intimacy, Sociability, Affection	Disregard, Loneliness, Seclusion, Rejection
Mastery	Competency, Persistence, Creativity, Resolution	Inadequacy, Attenuation, Stagnation, Resignation
Independence	Autonomy, Confidence, Inner Control, Prevalence	Submission, Self-Doubt, Powerlessness, Inferiority
Generosity	Trust, Giving, Sharing, Empathy	Distrust, Selfishness, Narcissism, Apathy

We know which dimensions take up the most time and energy and those on which we would like to focus more attention. We also recognize that certain people possess a way of harmony that distinguishes them as being "more at peace with themselves and their world." Whether or not they are truly living this "Beauty way" remains a question, but the air of contentment, a presence, or the peace of mind that does indeed characterize certain people speaks the language of harmony. The true question is raised: How do we attain this sense of harmony within our own lives? The Inner Circle has a unique answer for every person. Specific exercises are recommended to strengthen or weaken each of the Four Dimensions present within ourselves. Yet before entering into this process of rebalancing we must first fully understand how these Dimensions play out in our everyday lives. To do that we can consider the following teachings: the Rule of Opposites, the Source, Deflection, the Circle of Learning, the Transition Circle, and Purpose and Direction.

THE RULE OF OPPOSITES

While walking in the Smokey Mountains one brisk fall day, an elder Medicine Man came upon a young Indian man sitting on the ground. Sensing that the young man was troubled by something, he asked, "Why is it that you are sitting here like this?"

"I am sitting here because I do not know which way to go," answered the young man.

"You do know the path of the Sun," replied the elder.

"Yes," said the young man, "but I do not know which direction I am to follow."

The elder Medicine Man sat with the young Indian man and reminded him of the lessons offered by the each of the Four Directions. He suggested that the young man spend four days and four nights fasting in order to seek the lessons in each of the different directions, one for each night. On the morning of the fifth day, the young man was to nourish his body and resume his journey in the direction that seemed best as revealed in his vision.

"How will I know if I am moving in the right direction?" asked the young man.

"Home is wherever you are," said the elder, smiling. "Stay in harmony and balance in your life's journey, and may the spirits guide you as you walk the path of Good Medicine."

Choice drives the circles we follow and the cycles that we live out. Life consists of a series of choices that present us with challenges to be fulfilled or ignored, consequences to be accepted or rejected. *There's a right way and a wrong way; somewhere in between lies the truth.*

The concept of choice is central to the Native American

way of life. It is the very nature of things that for every choice there is a non-choice. Choosing one thing also means not choosing another thing. The choice of accepting or rejecting also means a decision to accept or reject the consequences of that choice. Even guidance or advice is a matter of choice, something that is learned early on in our development. To be forced into a decision or manipulated "for our own good" is similar to conjuring or influencing.

Influence and interference are considered as taking choice away, which is not acceptable in the Native American way. An elder told of a young man who borrowed something special from a friend's Medicine bag, with the intent of returning it when done. When ready to return this special thing, he could not find it. Frantic, he went to a Medicine Man to ask him to help find it. The Medicine Man asked where he got it and why he was using it. The young man told him the entire story. The Medicine Man asked him to go back to his friend and ask to see the special thing that he took from him without telling him he took it, which the young man did without hesitation. His friend was surprised, but opened his Medicine bag to show him the special object, which to the young man's amazement was there! How could this be?

The young man went immediately back to the Medicine Man and asked how he returned it. The Medicine Man explained that everything in life had choice, and the special object chose to return itself to the safety and comfort of the friend's Medicine bag. While it was lost to the young man, the special object was not lost, only finding its way. The young man, still puzzled, gifted the elder with tobacco and gifted his friend as well.

The old ones taught us that when a person says something they usually mean the opposite of that, unless it is a truth. The question is, who's truth is it? A person came to Doc Amoneeta Sequoyah once and said, " I am having problems with colitis, and I don't want to take the prescription given to me. It has side effects, and I was told that you had a Medicine for it."

Doc said, "Well, let me think about it." He went back into his home and continued to drink some of the coffee I made for him.

The woman was very anxious and finally said, "I have to go, I'm in a hurry."

Doc looked at her and said, "You may have what the white doctor called 'colitis,' but what you really have is 'being in too big a hurry disease.' If you don't slow down you will have something worst than that, if you live long enough." She did not need to hurry, she needed to slow down. The disease was not the problem; she was the problem.

The Rule of Opposites teaches us to listen carefully to what people say, and not to get caught up in their demands for themselves.

Opposites sometimes enter our lives in the form of discrepant thoughts, feelings, or behaviors. Insomniacs seem to concern themselves with falling asleep to the point that precisely that goal which they seek becomes sadly unattainable. Indeed, the insomniac may be faced with difficult circumstances that call on him to make some decision not wanting to be made, resulting in sleeplessness. Likewise, we are sometimes faced with a decision between the unacceptable and the undesirable.

This is a natural part of living. Any decision is bound to involve many complicated factors and options that must be weighed carefully against each other. However, it is our own inner strength that benefits from the effort required to willingly choose among them, and furthermore, to seek resolve after having made a choice.

We sometimes create our own opposites, wherein we become the very source of our discomfort. Hypochondriacs visit the doctor time and time again only to hear that there is nothing wrong, leaving them more determined than before to prove that there is something wrong, which in itself may result in illness. In this instance the hypochondriac has created the very condition she was seeking so desperately to avoid.

Again, the lesson of opposites is that of choice. Though two things may seem completely opposite, both are true. We may look at a coin that has two sides—heads and tails. The two sides seem separate and unrelated. If we flip the coin it will land on either heads or tails. What we often fail to remember, however, is that the two opposing sides are both part of the same coin, just as any two opposites are often part of the same truth.

In making our choices we must have the presence of mind to recognize the underlying truths that are involved. This calls upon us to question our assumptions in a search for whatever truths may not be readily evident to us. For example, guilt, which is resentment of one's self for any number of reasons, could just as easily be resentment of others in the form of anger. There is a fine line between the two, although the energy invested may be the same for both. Instead of searching for reasons to justify our opposites or blaming others for our discrepancies, maybe we should examine the energy of that discrepancy, questioning the underlying truths and ultimately clarifying our own assumptions.

Some people who cry when they are upset also cry when they are overwhelmed with joy. Again, there is a fine line. Likewise, asking "What did you say?" implies the question, "What did you not say?" Both are equally important and, indeed, part of the same truth. The difference simply lies in a personal choice that is made and a perspective that is chosen based upon personal assumptions.

The same holds true for people who concentrate their efforts on avoiding something rather than working toward something. It becomes important for us to clarify the assumptions upon which we are acting rather than focusing so much energy on simply justifying our actions. Being "right" and being true are two different things. Very often our thinking centers around what is "right and wrong" rather than what is true.

The Inner Circle is built on opposites and moves according the Rule of Opposites: **independence** is an extension of **belonging; generosity** is an extension of **mastery**. The eagle feather teaches us about the Rule of Opposites, about everything being divided into two ways. The more one is caught up in the physical, or the West, the more one has to go in the opposite direction of East, or the spiritual, to get balance. And it works the other way too—you can't focus on the spiritual to the exclusion of the physical. We require harmony in all Four Directions.

If we consider for a moment the eagle feather with its light and dark colors, one could argue that the dark colors are far more beautiful and, therefore, naturally more valuable (or vice versa). Regardless of which colors are said to be more beautiful, or necessary, or valuable, the truth is this: both colors come from the same feather, both are true, they are connected, and it takes both to fly.

Balance describes a way of being in which all elements, pain as well as pleasure, serve a useful and necessary function. We create our own balance, and cause our own imbalance, with choices. Many of us, upon being asked, would respond that what we are seeking most in life is some form of happiness.

We may have different concepts of what happiness is or how to achieve it, but our final goal would probably be to choose to be happy.

Ironically, the very selection of happiness as a goal prevents its attainment. As Viktor Frankl writes in his book *Man's Search for Meaning*, "Happiness cannot be pursued; it must ensue." This is true to the extent that happiness is a frame of mind that results from having a reason to be happy. Frankl similarly adds, "If you want anyone to laugh you have to provide him with reason, e.g., you have to tell him a joke." You cannot expect people to laugh by simply asking them to laugh, or by asking them to make themselves laugh.

Some decisions are not decisions at all, or are they? When armchair philosophers pose the age-old question, "Is the glass half-empty or is it half-full?" the Rule of Opposites would meanwhile ask, "What size is the glass?" Thus, the Rule of Opposites reminds us how important it is to ask the right questions. When we are faced with decisions between the unacceptable and the undesirable, it might be important to ask ourselves, "Does this situation represent a deeper lesson for me than what I see right now?" rather than simply focusing on a seemingly no-win decision between "this and that." Our cycles of self-defeat are borne of the belief that we have no choice available to us, or that we must fight the choices we do have rather than create new ones by trusting ourselves and looking beyond face value. This is the origin of internal discrepancies which, as we shall see, are fueled by choices made with regard to our innermost fears. Looking at our options as separate and unrelated often leads us into the unfortunate trap of not understanding situations for what they *really* may be.

Asking the right questions and having the courage to

receive the corresponding answers often bridges the gap between *what we expect to be* and *what is*. In a one-directional approach to living, our goal is to feel more pleasure, less pain; more happiness and less sadness; more positive and less negative. In a two-directional approach prescribed by the Rule of Opposites, our goal is to find meaning in *both* pleasure and pain; in *both* happiness and sadness; and in *both* positive and negative experiences. A shift in thinking allows us to seek a balance by realizing that everything serves a useful and valued function in our lives. This shift in thinking also allows us the room to fully consider the choices available to us. By understanding our own truths we eliminate any need for the existence of discrepancies.

In summary, the Rule of Opposites honors us with several important lessons.

1. Opposites are extensions of themselves, like two opposing hands of the same body; one side of the coin/question/ equation implies the other.

2. We create our own opposites (discrepancies), wherein we become the source of our difficulty.

3. Everything serves a useful and important function in our lives.

4. Asking the right *questions*, instead of asking for the right *answers*, allows us to recognize function rather than effect.

5. Questioning our assumptions leads to the recognition of underlying truths and choices made.

6. Understanding underlying truths eliminates any need for the existence of discrepancy.

7. We are free to balance ourselves as we see fit.

For an example of how to use the Rule of Opposites in one's life, view the "Reframing" technique in part 3 (p. 157). This strategy enables us to change a frame of reference by introducing a slightly different meaning to a particular situation. A similar strategy is employed in the Crazy Dog technique (p. 167), which explores the consequences of opposite actions or reactions by having participants do the opposite of their normal, expected behavior.

FINDING THE SOURCE

Fear is a feeling without reality. The Old Ones taught us that we could make fear a reality by our choices. We look one higher than us for guidance; otherwise we might live in constant fear. The Cherokee way is to not look fear in the face but to allow fear to look itself in the face, while we recognize fear as just fear and then go on with our lives.
—ABE LOSSIAH, CHEROKEE ELDER

The possibility of choice can be viewed as creating hope in one situation and anxiety in another. It is often said that the person who has a deep fear of drowning will be the most likely to drown simply by virtue of the fear that she or he has chosen. Thrashing about in the water the person panics and tires to the point of drowning in an attempt to fight that very outcome. In shock and dismay, all those who knew the person will mutter among themselves how careful so-and-so always was, taking every precaution to avoid such an untimely end.

Fear and doubt are natural parts of our human experience that lie on the opposite side of love, acceptance, purpose, and direction. Who among us hasn't experienced fear and doubt? No one. This is a normal part of living and growing.

We have all experienced a fear of choosing the wrong thing to say or do, of not doing well, or of not being accepted by others. All of these fears come from an anticipation of what we *do not* know. This is the other side of possibility at the source of the Inner Circle—the fear of the unknown.

What we *do* know can serve as a source of balance, purpose, and direction in our lives. However, according to the Rule of Opposites, in the absence of courage and truth what we *do not* know can lead to anticipation, anxiety, and uncertainty that results in perceptions of helplessness or ambivalence. Imbalance and disharmony very quickly ensue. In the absence of perceived choices, we deteriorate. We buckle under, giving in to the stresses of everyday life and to the ever-present demands placed upon us by our conditions. We develop mental lapses in concentration and functioning, spiritual emptiness, and physical ailments of the heart, stomach, or head.

To a certain degree an acceptable level of challenge in our lives provides the necessary pull toward meaningful experiences and truths that contribute to our overall sense of well-being. This challenge also comes in the form of fears that serve the natural purpose of protecting us from harm. But taken to an extreme, these fears can overwhelm us and inhibit our inner balance to the point of affecting choice and the perception of choice.

There was a man who was once so afraid of finding the truth that he did not look for it. He passed on in fear. Another man listened to the teachings of the elders, and he knew there would be fear as he was seeking the answers to life. He was guided by Great White Eagle, who caught him before he fell off the mountain when he was a small child walking away from his mother, who was working in the planting field. He went into the woods alone while playing, trusting that the fox was his friend and to hear a tree talking to him, telling him not to be afraid, but just to smile and sing his song-chant. He went to the edge of himself and found that he could end it all or work through his adversity as a young person.

He became an adult and faced his fear of survival as he grew older and taught others not to fear fear. In his last moments of life he met Great White Eagle again at the mountain's edge. He was carried off into the sky without fear, for fear was his partner in life.

The source of many of our problems is fear. As an elder said, "The source of harmony is not having disharmony. The source of balance is not having imbalance. The source of our problems is to not make it a problem." We can think of source as the point of origin or the creator of something. The "old ones" would call it a beginning of something that has an end by going back to the beginning again and doing a clearing-way for the way of right relationship with all things. To find the answer, the source, find the right question to lead you to the beginning or source of the "opportunity," rather than to the problem.

The Four Directions provide us a guide to follow in looking at spiritual, natural, physical, and mental influences or interferences within the Universal Circle that can be helpmates in asking the right question to get to the source of the opportunity for new choices in our lives.

In the East we treasure that sense of belonging that comes from our relationships with others and a unity among people. We like to feel a part of something or have some place to call home, especially in the hearts of others. It is here that we find the acceptance and sharing that distinguishes us as social beings. It is also here that an ever-present fear of rejection or abandonment lingers with the ultimate anticipation of being isolated and alone.

In the South we discover a sense of mastery over ourselves and over select parts of our environment. We learn certain abilities and develop others that test our creativity and resilience. Here we enjoy the empowerment that goes along with being able to do something. This is where we choose to persist, or to give up. This is where our fear of failure resides with the possibility of not being "good enough" to handle things or to perform them well enough. Ultimately we anticipate the awesome responsibility involved in doing something and doing it well.

In the West we seek an answer to the question "Who am I?" Here is where we search ourselves in an attempt to define what our strengths are and what it is we believe in. These things mark us as unique and autonomous. We look for our individuality and, in striving for that, develop the confidence that is necessary to successfully confront life and living. This is also where we seek to avoid that fear of regret that comes with definition and separation from "the whole." The searching, the making of decisions about ourselves, others, and the world around us, brings with it a certain sense of finality that we begrudgingly anticipate. Ultimately this is where we recognize not only the finality of decisions but our own finality as well: mortality.

In the North we practice the openness to experience in order to learn more about our lives and the process of living. We thrive on understanding and accountability, and on being able to give to others, not only of our possessions but also of our knowledge and of ourselves. We recognize the experiences of others and relate to them willingly based on our own. It is here that opening ourselves and trusting reminds us of that fear of vulnerability that remains a constant threat to our "safety" if we let it be. We anticipate the inequity that could arise from giving and sharing of ourselves in ways that leave us somewhat unprotected.

All in all our fears remind us to keep ourselves from harm's way, but they can just as easily interfere with our choices and our harmony if we let them. A woman who is afraid of being hit by a car refuses to cross the street. The chances of her not being hit by a car may be better; but she will, as a result of not facing her fear, be confined to places without street crossings. The chances are just as good that her Inner Circle will, to some extent, be disrupted through the diminished possibilities available to her. But then again, this is the price we pay for avoidance. *It's one thing to know your limitations and quite another to hide behind them.*

How many people trudge through life believing that they don't have a choice in the matter, it wasn't their fault, they didn't do anything, it's a disease, or they just can't help it? These are all choices that significantly affect a person's harmony and balance. These are all choices made out of fear, doubt, or uncertainty based on the avoidance of fears. The source of our harmony can just as easily be the source of our disharmony.

For a better understanding of the choices you make, and how these choices influence your thoughts, feelings and behavior, refer to the Sourcing technique in part 3 (p. 156).

DEFLECTION

Anticipation of the pain can be worse than the pain itself. For example, we may or may not feel the smooth sensation of a yellow jacket curiously probing and lightly brushing our skin for the sake of a fear swelling up in us over the threat of being stung. Yet the Rule of Opposites tells us that the source of pain could just as easily be a source of learning. Similarly, that which is a source of fear could just as easily be a source of courage and understanding.

Our insecurities, our fears, our feelings of helplessness and frustration all feed on themselves through our decision to let them by following these paths of disharmony. The so-called symptoms many people develop can be traced to the point of origin at which a decision is made to either face a fear or to avoid it. As we cycle through our Inner Circle we reaffirm the presence or absence of a dimension through daily activities: sharing, cooperation, exploration, introspection, definition, reflection, or teaching. These activities serve as a broad "umbrella" for such endeavors as work, intimate relationships, exercise, eating, leisure, and so on. Ironically, the very same activities that serve to balance us can also serve to take us off balance us through a process known as *deflection*.

As we move through each of the Four Dimensions we are confronted with the challenge of facing or avoiding our fear in that direction. The activities we choose may be the same either way, but the intention at the very heart of it all is what counts. This intention is known as the point of origin.

If we consider the arrowhead for a moment we see that it has two edges that are opposite yet the same. Both edges are a part of the same arrowhead but on opposite sides. Whereas one edge may represent the taking of life, the opposite edge can represent the giving of life. In the old days, in order to preserve his life and the life of his family a hunter had to take the life of an animal, remembering always to give thanks for the animal's willingness to offer its life. The arrowhead symbolizes this dichotomy between such opposites as life and death.

By analogy, if we take an arrowhead to represent one of our fears, one edge represents balancing and the other deflection. The tip of the arrowhead, then, represents the point of origin, or the decision that is made to either face the fear or avoid it. Facing the fear sends us on a path of balancing as we fulfill the Dimension bounded by that arrowhead, resulting in a choice toward courage and wisdom. Avoiding the fear results in imbalance and disharmony. As an elder said, "Create your own path that balances you in your own way, with choices that create harmony with your friends and family. You will see fear disappear and confidence replace fear."

To sum it up briefly, each of the four fears (rejection, failure, regret, and vulnerability) follows a path of imbalance through deflection or avoidance. The result: the corresponding dimension acts as a source of imbalance for us. The opposite edge, the one within the circle, strengthens us by allowing the corresponding dimension to function as a source of balance. This is accomplished by making the choice to face the fear in that direction, which helps us to grow and to develop courage and understanding.

For instance, in the direction of East we seek a sense of belonging through relationships with others. The arrowhead, or fear, in that direction is rejection. One way of balancing with a sense of belonging is through establishing a relationship with another person that can provide an opportunity for mutual caring and support in spite of our fear of rejection. Essentially we can use the fear of rejection to recognize limitations and make "good" choices for ourselves. This contributes to a heightened sense of belonging, and the resulting harmony and courage that grows out of inner balance.

However, we could just as well enter into a relationship out of a fear of rejection and isolation, thereby using the relationship to avoid our fears through deflection. The resulting imbalance would most likely affect not only our Inner Circle and sense of well-being, but the sincerity and functioning of the relationship as well.

We can do things the hard way, or we can do things the easy way. The process of deflection is similar to reading a book about living—only instead of reading the book you acquire the Cliff Notes. After all, think how much time it would take, how much trouble it would be, how painful an experience it would be to read the whole book! So you read the Cliff Notes with the expectation that you will receive the full effect of having read the entire book from cover to cover. You will probably have a general feel for the plot and several basic themes. However, one fact still remains: you will not have read the book, you will not have experienced the book, and though you may have acquired a working knowledge of the book, you will not have carried its wisdom with you. Most importantly, you will probably do the exact same thing when it comes time to read another book. If it worked once why not try it again, right? Besides, think of all the trouble and anguish it saved you!

An imbalance of the Inner Circle through deflection very often leads to eventual feelings of helplessness or ambivalence by depleting a person's source of inner strength and well-being. An excess of any activity or path can lead to an exaggeration of one direction to the exclusion of the opposite direction.

Imbalance means that there is an exaggeration or absence of a particular dimension in the Inner Circle. For example, the process of deflection can cause a person to have too much or too little independence. The main imbalances caused by deflection are outlined below.

DEFLECTION IMBALANCES

An excess of:

Belonging (East)	results in	**overdependence**
Mastery (South)	results in	**overachievement**
Introspection (West)	results in	**self-absorption**
Generosity (North)	results in	**martyrdom**

THE CIRCLE OF LEARNING

Traditionally in Cherokee tribal culture there were Circles of Learning that were much like "focus groups" today. These circles offered special opportunities to share concepts or ideas beyond the everyday activities and skills learned to survive. Instead of bringing together the greatest minds or the most skilled persons, an invitation would go out to specific people who demonstrated unusual talent, as recommended by the elders of each clan. Also invited were elders who had great skills as orators, or were skilled hunters or warriors. Every participant was equally respected in the Circle of Learning.

Unlike the scientific forums or "skills workshops" of today, which the "masters" teach, in the Circle of Learning the masters would listen and relearn at the side of a beloved elder. As an elder said, "Sometimes the simplest thinking can have profound creative impact. The question might be how we can make a better arrowhead or a stronger storage building to replace the traditional corn bin. We were a people with creative minds and opportunities provided by the Great One. We honored him by better serving our community and our environment."

An elder shared an example of how a clan of the Cherokee tribe had floods on the land of their ancestors along the Tuckasegee River near present day Bryson City, North Carolina. As the winter snows would melt there would be flash floods, and sometimes the river would decide its own course. The story goes that a circle of tribal members got together to decide what to do. A call went out to those who had ideas on how to avoid the flooding of the ancestor's place, an old village site of graves and a mound of spiritual significance to the people. There were a few that came forward but those had already been heard: move the clan and dig the remains. But disturbing the graves of the ancestors was not an option.

The "spiritual ones" sought guidance and the elder priest was called for wisdom. The elder priest called for the young people to come forward with their ideas. Two of those young people were Feather and Walkingstick. Both worked with the different woods for building sacred fires, building sturdy round houses.

In response to flooding, these young people created the Beaver Society, which spent many hours watching the beaver build dams to divert the water. As the story goes, it was the first dam built by the beavers and the Beaver Society to divert a part of the Tuckaseegee River "downstream from Governor's Island" near Bryson City.

The Circle of Learning pushes the circle of what is known and the comfort zone of the present day to seeking guidance from the ancestors or from the masters of Nature herself. Much was learned in these circles by watching animals in their natural habitat, or by engaging in "vision quests" to call upon the ancestors. There are many earlier stories of Circles of Learning that led to finding the "Enchanted Lake," the origin of Bigwitch, and the renewal of the old sacred ways for ceremonies. This is a way that a community can work with a historian, as an example, to find special things and events to re-create a portion of the past for the benefit of the future. The Circles of Learning can be originated by members of a community or church, concerned citizens, or any individual who wants to honor the culture and traditions that made us who we are today.

A good friend, Cherokee elder and Medicine Woman Pat DeAsis, is now retired from her position as the director of communications for the Indian Health Service. Her Medicine-way is to work with Circles of Learning to facilitate ideas and opportunities and "learning from the positive and negative lessons of life." What she did with her grandchildren and with so many of us as friends is what she called "making a memory." She learned the traditional lesson of learning, which is to take every experience as a teaching. She would say, "To have a positive experience you have to create a positive experience." She is a helper to young Indian women, assisting to them to "create a positive opportunity from a negative experience, to give you woman power."

Through the Circle of Learning we discover understanding and purpose. Both of these are crucial to inner balance and harmony.

THE TRANSITION CIRCLE

An elder said, "Things are going too fast these days. The young people don't have time to learn the stories from the elders, who have been replaced by computers. They are influenced by other cultures and teachings from all over the world. This is a good thing, but we are quickly losing our own culture. Many of them are coming back to the old ways to help deal with the obsessions of life: drugs, abuse, and the ills of today. I tell them, you have to understand that you are in a transitional society that changes with each new convenience. It is difficult to know what is good and bad anymore. Even our fears have changed. Even though I say these things, I envy my grandson who has such freedom that I never had. I also worry about him, 'cause he is in a circle that is moving too fast. At least he has a tradition to come back too, for now."

Life is one great circle of experiences. The process of living always involves something to learn, something to experience, something to understand. Each of us does it in different ways. There are both "good" experiences and "bad" ones, depending on individual interpretation. What we take away from each experience varies from situation to situation, time to time, and is simply a question of choice. Unfortunately, we sometimes get so caught up in troubling experiences that we are essentially unable to experience the satisfying ones. We are reminded of a simple truth: *Nobody can see good things if they are thinking only bad things.*

In a sense we do not allow ourselves to experience the good until we are ready, until we decide that whatever burden we are carrying is no longer worth carrying. Circumstances come and go; however, it is us who choose the shape, texture, flavor, and color of our own inner world.

Life is one great circle of transitions that reflects the path followed by the Sun. The Sun rises in the East (connection) and slowly works its way across the sky until finally setting in the West (separation), moving out of sight and remaining present only inside of us. In doing we discover our strengths, our interests, our beliefs. These discoveries define us as unique and relatively separate; they teach us about who we are (knowing). Knowing and self-knowledge results in the process of connection and relation with current and previous experiences; in a sense, we see the "light." Connection results in more doing, which leads to separation and introspection in an attempt to define and make sense out of what we know of ourselves as a whole. Following the departure of the Sun beneath the horizon we find time to reflect upon what wisdom has been given to us during the day.

We experience, grow, and undergo transitions that help us to grow even more. The Transition Circle shows us this dynamic process that, again, results in deepened levels of understanding and purpose. The Transitioning technique in part 3 (p. 151) provides a series of questions to draw awareness to the important transitions in our lives and incite discussion on how we handled these changes. This seeking of balance and harmony is crucial in a constantly shifting interaction between ourselves and our world.

PURPOSE AND DIRECTION

A Medicine Woman said, "It is important to give our grandchildren the room to grow, but be there to support them when they must know their true purpose in life. The old ways have guided us for many generations, but it loses some of its benefit in the dominant society. Our young people want to be more like the dominant society, and we must step back and allow that to happen. While some worry that we have lost our youth, I say that they will come back to the old ways as they find the ways of the other world don't fit them, or they really don't feel they fit there. I guess that is the way it should be. The important thing is for them to find their own Medicine-way."

Everyone has a "religion." Though the magnitude of commitment may vary from person to person, we all have a belief system, a code of ethics, a philosophy or a way of being that specifically orients us to the world in which we live. Every human being needs something to believe in. This is our "Medicine-way," which, guided by our innermost thoughts and feelings, is a "personal religion" requiring a great deal of conviction. We search for reasons for living, for doing the things that we do, for "things" being the way that they are. In the end we usually find what we're looking for.

Our Medicine-way guides our reactions and directs the decisions we make on a continual basis. In a sense this personal religion of ours creates a pathway along which we direct our lives. However we can never completely foresee what the future holds for us, nor do we ever truly "know" ourselves. Therefore the unknown determines the direction of our lives when we allow our fears to control our choices and, ultimately, our perceptions of choice.

Deep within each of us reside our own unique personal truths. Only when the doors of perception are opened and the limitations shed like a skin from our bodies will these truths be known in their fullest.

Know your strengths and use your limitations. There are many ways of fulfilling each of our inner dimensions. Though we may follow any number of paths toward learning or experiencing, natural fears in each of the Four Directions potentially bar us from fully knowing our personal truths. By confronting our fears in each of the Directions, we confront ourselves. Essentially, we recognize our limitations and realize our strengths. By doing so we seek to bridge the gaps within ourselves.

The paths we choose are very often a reflection of our Medicine-way, and help us to achieve whatever it is that we are seeking to achieve. Of course, this assumes that the path we choose is our own path of understanding, with our own spiritual way. Each of us has our Medicine-way, which integrates our choices and experiences in the Four Directions for harmony and balance.

In anticipation of the unknown—unfamiliar situations, something not yet encountered, or something to be avoided—we construct barriers and limitations, which only we can overcome. Ironically, the paths we choose can be employed to *avoid* challenges or to *meet* them. It is not our fears but we who decide the capacity in which our paths will function. In doing so we decide upon ourselves and on the meaning we give to our lives. Possibility, then, becomes a tool for the fulfillment of this meaning. *The worst thing about having so many choices is having to choose.*

Individual empowerment is probably one of the most widely sought after and yet least understood concepts of our time. Many people have wondered, "Why am I here?" or at minimum, "How can I best live my life?" Unfortunately, looking for the right answers by asking the wrong questions is a typical misunderstanding of the freedom we enjoy in the face of possibility.

Life is a gift, but living is something we must give ourselves. Living, too, involves practicing the strength to listen to our inner wisdom and to let others live as they so choose, without interference from us. But is this humanly impossible?

Fortunately it is our humanity that endows our lives not only with the capacity for *being* but also for *becoming*. Accepting responsibility for one's life without harboring feelings of resentment or false satisfaction is what many people collectively refer to as integrity, or "coming into your own." Undoubtedly, this is a difficult balance to strike, especially given our propensity to overlook the possibility that each of us possesses the answers to our own questions.

We all seek a purpose for our striving and a direction in which to move. Yet we may not wish to reach too deeply for fear of actually finding an answer, and thereby eliminating the question. Ultimately we fear that what we find will not be as great as hoped for, that our lives will have been wasted and our efforts futile. This is a profound dilemma faced by all of us at some point in our lives. This is the risk we take—or do not take. We look for an end to justify all of our means and efforts, and yet we fear that the end will be nothing more than that: an ending. This is the dichotomy of choice. And this is also the beauty of living—that vast array of possibilities that adorn our every thought and movement, washing our lives in a stream of meanings just waiting to be discovered.

Participants in search of their own purpose and direction will find the Four Directions technique in part 3 (p. 148) particularly helpful. Working together with others in a circle, individuals identify their present direction and explore where they would like to be in the future. The knowledge of the Four Dimensions is used to enhance one's self-awareness that will open the doors to rebalancing. Other useful exercises for those seeking guidance include the Guide (p. 180), the Mountain (p. 184), and the Sacred Path (p. 185).

8
Good Medicine Path

Once we have an understanding of the Four Dimensions and the Four Directions, we can use these tools for deciding a way to wellness that we call a Good Medicine Path. Once we are comfortable with our own Medicine-way we can better appreciate how the physical, spiritual, mental, and natural aspects of our life can help us with a wellness focus. What is the best way in which to live our lives? How do we go about living so that when our time has passed we do not feel regret over what we have done, who we have been, and where we have gone? What is that unmistakable sense of contentment that touches our lives at various times, however small, and from where does it come? How may we rid ourselves of the pain and suffering and uncertainty that is so much a part of the human condition?

Many of those who speak of harmony ordinarily do so in reference to music. Each of the instruments—the string instruments such as violin, cello, bass, guitar; percussion instruments such as drums, bells, cymbals, bongos; wind instruments such as flute, trumpet, oboe, clarinet, trombone, saxophone; and voice—all of these instruments separately carry a particular sound with a limited range. However, taken together in different combinations, or in one extravagant symphony, these instruments are capable of producing harmonious music powerful enough to move anyone beyond belief. Moreover, the music varies according to the mood and ambience of changing conditions or experiences.

How does this relate to us? We create ourselves out of silence or out of noise, and we choose our supreme rhythms by which we move with different shades of emotion and thought. Hence, we are music. We select our own instruments from each of the paths, producing shifting levels of **belonging, mastery, independence,** and **generosity**. We balance their sounds against one another in a way that creates a divine experience of harmony and wellness. We respond to the challenge of having no sheet music to guide us in the melodies we produce, and rely on our knowledge of the instruments' capabilities and combinations. We choose the style of presentation and we choose the measure.

Harmony is created when all Four Dimensions—**belonging, mastery, independence,** and **generosity**—are synchronized and comfortably balanced within a person. This means that each of the Dimensions offset one another in an individually acceptable way. The path to wellness leads through harmony; if wellness is the goal of our lives, then harmony is the means. Harmony, in turn, is that state of being that results from an undisrupted and unbroken Inner Circle in which **belonging, mastery, independence,** and **generosity** are chosen without regard to avoidance of personal fears and uncertainty. *The only true limitations that are placed upon us come from within.*

It is believed that a person can "walk in harmony" despite conditions or circumstances that affect the mind, body, and spirit. As Carol Locust expresses, "It is not the events that happen to a person, but his or her responses to those events that create harmony." She goes on to say that "every human

chooses his responses, and thus chooses harmony or disharmony." Therefore, harmony is a choice between courage and
avoidance. Having the courage to confront oneself, to know
oneself and be willing to face one's fears even in the presence
of less than favorable conditions, this unique balance of self-
awareness, life purpose, and inner strength comes from a personal balance among one's inner dimensions. Here, too, the
willingness to face one's fears becomes crucial to maintaining
personal balance. It is not an easy task, which in the end makes
it all that more precious.

Courage is an attitude toward life and the process of living
that springs from deep within us. It is a strength that allows us
to be our own person and can carry us well beyond our limitations, fears, suffering, and ultimately ourselves. Courage is a
choice. It is the culmination of a lifetime's worth of choices.

When we know ourselves, when we have balanced our Inner Circle, when we have recognized our purpose, and when
we have chosen the courage to face our fears, that is when we
have chosen the path of harmony, and that is where we will
find wellness.

It goes without saying that the disruption of harmony results in unwellness. Intuitively we realize this truth. Illness is
considered by Native Americans to be needed by some people
for invaluable experience and learning. The Native American
perspective on illness and the significance of harmony is well
described by Carol Locust in her book *American Indian Beliefs
Concerning Health and Unwellness:*

> Indians believe that each individual chooses to make him-
> self well or to make himself unwell. If one stays in harmony,
> keeps all the tribal laws and all the sacred laws, one's spirit

will be so strong that negativity will be unable to affect it. If one chooses to let anger or jealousy or self-pity control him he has created disharmony for himself. Being in control of one's emotional responses is necessary if one is to remain in harmony. Once harmony is broken, however, the spiritual self is weakened and one becomes vulnerable to physical illness, mental and/or emotional upsets, and the disharmony projected by others.

Individual decisions play a large role in creating wellness or unwellness. Unwellness can take any number of forms, including physical, spiritual, or mental illness. However, the severity of disharmony and reasons for such are determined primarily by the choices made and reactions chosen.

Every thought and every action counts. In effect, we are responsible for our wellness and for our unwellness. Something as simple as suppressed anger or fear is enough to create disharmony that will in time result in unwellness, whether in the form of ulcers, fatigue, high blood pressure, or another such condition. Moreover, our harmony or disharmony extends to those around us, as we each are a part of the greater circle—the Universal Circle.

Though we are connected, it is understood that no two people are alike. One person's harmony may be considered disharmony for another person. Full Circle is based on the notion that every person is different, and that we each have our own unique form of harmony. As such, Full Circle asks the following questions:

1. What does it take for us to live with ourselves?

2. What does it take for us to live with others?

3. What does it take for us to live in our surroundings?

4. What does it take for us to live meaningful lives?

These are questions that we each ask ourselves in the act of living out our lives. Full Circle captures this process of living by showing us the lessons of human nature. How we specifically go about living is strictly up to us. Oftentimes people who seek help are doing so because the lessons of the balanced circle have eluded them in some way. They search for answers to their unanswered questions and look to eliminate feelings of helplessness or ambivalence. Experiencing discrepancy in their lives, people seek help as a result of disharmony, disarray, and distress.

Disharmony is the result of a gap between what we expect to happen and what is. This disharmony usually takes the form of so-called negative emotional responses, such as depression, anger, confusion, guilt, or fear. How we choose to interpret discrepancy is up to us. Even happiness is a reaction to a discrepancy between what one expected and what actually is—reality ends up exceeding what was expected. When expectations and reality are in synch we feel a sense of contentment; we experience harmony.

If synchronizing expectations and reality is what brings about contentment, then achieving harmony is simply a matter of bridging the gap between the two, right? Yes. However, when faced with a discrepancy most people do not choose to bridge this gap—most people try to change reality rather than change their own expectations. But reality is difficult to change, especially when it involves multiple factors that we have little or no control over. What we can control are our own expectations, as well as our reactions and interpretations. This can work to our advantage if we let it.

The first step is realizing that there is a discrepancy between what we expect and what is. This is usually pretty easy to detect, since it is in our nature to react and reactions are signs. The next step is to determine how to bridge the gap between expectations and reality, becoming aware of all of the options and weighing them against one another. The final step is actually doing it. Many times this may include altering one's expectations, making harmony the ultimate goal. The entire process requires courage, clarity, and openness. We must realize what we are choosing and whether or not it is truly what we want—this is the process of awareness. In order to be well we must sometimes walk the path of healing—this is the process of patience and openness. In order to stay well, we must always recognize the source of that wellness, and do what we can to tap in to it.

Choices for wellness have to be examined in each of the Four Directions by the question, "What does it take for me to prevent disease and to have wellness in my life?" Of course we all realize that certain habits, such as smoking, are harmful to our health, or that we need a certain number of hours of sleep to feel good.

Usually the physical aspects of the West Medicine we learn about from school, television, and the news media. What about our spiritual wellness? Do we belong to a group that has our choice of beliefs and do we follow a way of life that we feel supports our spiritual well-being?

We encourage people to find that group, church, or belief system that is comforting and supportive of the individual and the family. This should fit your way of life. Of course, earlier American Indians had a way of life where ceremonies provided the sacredness and spirituality taught by the ancestors. Other religious beliefs were introduced, which today are integrated with American Indian churches and programs that include the Indian language, songs, and flute music as part of the regular service. Many people from different religious groups or belief systems come to the Full Circle gatherings. We always tell the participants, "Take what fits in your lifestyle and beliefs and leave the rest behind." It is your choice for a Good Medicine path of spirituality to seek harmony and balance.

Natural wellness of the South is being able to enjoy life, activities with family, and finding things to do that are enjoyable. Traditional activities included ball games, dances, and coming together for food. Today we enjoy a fish fry or a community dinner that is a family, clan, or tribal outing. The same is true for most any community. For the natural activities we enjoy an outing at a river, such as the Oconalufta or Tuckaseegee Rivers. At Full Circle gatherings we always enjoy "finding a special rock" at Smokemont or Collins Creek. A family could enjoy the same locations in Cherokee, North Carolina. Of course, any park where you can get outside and sit under a tree or just lie on Mother Earth is relaxing. Just get outside, even if planting flowers or a tree, and allow yourself to accept wellness in breathing and communicating with nature as Good Medicine.

Physical wellness of the West is about eating the right foods and taking supplements to compensate for the lack of nutrition in our foods and diet. There is so much good information out there that anyone can find a teacher or a website that assists with disease prevention. The traditional lesson is to eat fresh fruits, nuts, and salads for what an elder called "alive energy." While we will not say much here, we do encourage you to eat and live a life of Good Medicine to ensure "the best

you can feel naturally with natural foods and plant helpers."
If you do have a disease, learn as much about how to take care
of yourself and live with it as you can. Ask yourself, what am I
learning from this experience? As an elder said, "Learn to eat
and live right for the relationship with all things within the
Universal Circle. The plants and other helpers are there for
you, but you must search it out for yourself. We learned these
things from our ancestors."

North Medicine teaches us Good Medicine for calming
our systems during stress and using the plants to make into
teas for a relaxing sleeptime. Our ancestors taught us these
things. Much of this plant Medicine can be found in the book
entitled *Medicine of the Cherokee* by the same authors, as well as
The Cherokee Herbal by J. T. Garrett. If you cannot get out into
nature to find some quiet healing, then read *Meditations with
the Cherokee* by J. T. Garrett.

Healing may be thought of as a cure or treatment today.
Traditionally, healing was a way to restore our body or our
spiritual self to balance. This entire book is in some way about
healing. Everything in the traditional teachings included a
healing-way. The remainder of this book will introduce us to
a process that allows healing and a way to communicate
through a "talking circle," as well as exercises and techniques
adopted from traditional ways for healing.

PART THREE
The Healing-Way in Full Circle

9
Rebalancing

*In Cherokee Medicine you don't look at what's wrong
with a person, but what a person has been doing
wrong in their families and life.*
—Doc Amoneeta Sequoyah,
Cherokee Medicine elder

Making the judgment that there is something wrong with a person inevitably takes away choice. Taking away choice means taking away the opportunities for growth, for change, and for the courage to meet life's demands with an open heart and an open mind. Choice is the very lifeblood by which we truly live. It is the path that leads us beyond our limitations and our fears. The perceived absence of choice creates the downward-spiraling pathway known as "mental illness." Full Circle views choice as being at the heart of the internal conficts we experience in life, and it wields choice as a source of change, drawing on the human capacity for strength and perseverance. The choices we make affect the integrity of our Inner Circle.

The Full Circle approach to healing and wellness centers around helping people work toward change in and with a group. Full Circle "zeros in" on the underlying dynamics involved with the difficulties being experienced as well as the difficulties themselves. It is important that the so-called symptoms *and* the causes of a person's conflict both be examined, because they are deeply interrelated. The following assumptions are basic to the Full Circle process:

> Wellness varies according to the Four Dimensions of **belonging, mastery, independence,** and **generosity**.

> People experience difficulties related to disharmony among these Four Dimensions.

> People are what they are because of the decisions and choices they make on a continuously experiential basis.

> People have the power to change if they want to change.

Opposites are extensions of themselves—the arrowhead and the eagle feather again remind us of this lesson. **Independence** is an extension of **belonging; generosity** is an extension of **mastery**. Taken together, these Four Dimensions form the foundation for our balance or imbalance, harmony or disharmony, wellness or unwellness. Truly we all need someone to love, something to do, something to believe in, and something to look forward to. Our humanity implores the adequate presence of all Four Dimensions, and presents us with challenges to fulfill them in the form of fears. All Four Dimensions exist within the circle; the fears implicit within those Dimensions can serve to reaffirm the integrity of our Inner Circle.

Many times in our lives we attempt to avoid our innermost fears through a process known as deflection, and so we choose paths of imbalance and disharmony. The result of this disharmony is an exaggeration or an absence of certain of our Dimensions, a state of imbalance eventually leading to unwellness.

The path leading to the restoration of harmony is the very

same one that resulted in disharmony in the first place; however, rebalancing requires that the direction of one's choice be reversed. In coming back to balance a person resolves to confront his or her inner fears rather than focusing on avoiding them. A shift in thinking allows us to seek a balance by realizing that everything serves a useful and valued function in our lives: our goal is to find meaning in *both* pleasure and pain; in *both* happiness and sadness; and in *both* positive and negative experiences.

The process of rebalancing is an attempt to restore a person to harmony by balancing out the Four Dimensions, using a person's fears as a vehicle for change. Choice is the means by which this is accomplished.

People who enter the group process want to work on change and are willing to help others to do the same. Full Circle provides a way for humanity to draw on a unique approach to learning, experiencing, growing, and rebalancing based on Native American ways of looking at the cosmos, or Universal Circle. In a Native American worldview it is believed that a single life may be composed of many symbolic deaths and rebirths, which are an inevitable part of the life cycle. The process of death, transformation, and rebirth comprises a basic metaphor for all of life. A continual forming and reforming characterizes the many transformations that lead to growth. Life is the process of growing and should be welcomed as such.

Little has been written about Native American teachings and their application to such professional fields as health, education, counseling, social work, psychology, psychiatry, and numerous other specialty areas. By providing information, techniques, and exercises based on this unique set of cultural experiences and wisdom, it is hoped that a new understanding may be forged, that a new way will be offered, inviting all of our brothers and sisters to walk the path of "wellness."

Full Circle teachings provide a seven-step process to rebalancing, or "clearing-way," modeled after the Sweat Lodge Ceremony, a ceremony practiced for thousands of years by Native Americans. The Sweat Lodge Ceremony serves to purify those undergoing any sort of transformation or healing. As with the Sweat Lodge Ceremony, the Full Circle teachings take place within a four-step progression of entering, "crossing over," purifying, and emerging. We'll describe those phases now in the context of the Sweat Lodge Ceremony and come back to them in greater detail as the Full Circle teachings are explored.

The first step to entering the "sweat" is to be prepared by fasting and with prayers, and by that to have permission to enter the sweat lodge. Earlier long houses of the southeastern tribes had "sweats" built into the tribal way of living and with the change of seasons. As one elder said, "Entering [the sweat] is not just getting into the sometimes small and crowded space of a lodge. It is similar to going into another world. First your heart starts beating fast, then the heat engulfs you as you enter until you relax and breathe at a comfortable rate. You have now entered the present, past, and future. You are ready for guidance." This is what we call phase I: Entrance.

There is a threshold in the closed space—touching Mother Earth and feeling the heat—when there is a sense of calm. One stops some level of thoughts to finally get to a place of calm. This is what we call phase II: Threshold.

At some point while in the sweat one actually starts feeling the purging of toxins from the body. Sometimes one can feel slightly faint or giddy as the body adjusts to the heat and starts to release negative energy, as well as feeling some level of dehydration or stimulation of the body and its systems. This is what we call phase III: Purification.

Those leading the sweats may differ on how often you stay inside the sweat lodge and how many times you come out and enter again, how much you hydrate, and whether you take "healing drinks" with herbal mixtures. Finally, with guidance, one comes out of the sweat for a cold plunge, some kind of rinsing of the body with clean water. This is what we call phase IV: Emergence.

THE SACRED JOURNEY

At this point you might ask why someone would want to go through the Full Circle teachings. Full Circle is a journey, traditionally referred to as "the Sacred Journey," that was used as an initiation for young Medicine members being trained in the lessons of the Old Wisdom. Very few took part in this sacred journey, and much of what was taught came in pieces that would be transmited by different Medicine Men or elders of the tribe. These lessons were known usually by animal or bird names, such as the Crow Medicine Society or the Deer Medicine Society. (Medicine was known as *nv wa ti,* pronounced as "nah wah tea.") The teachings included song-chants, prayer-chants, activities for family participation, and teachings about plants and other natural items such as feathers and crystals used in the sacred Medicine.

In the traditional way, the "leader" of such a journey is humble and acts as a facilitator, rather than forging ahead with some agenda. In traditional groups for discussion, teaching, healing, or just coming together to decide something, the premise is to facilitate ideas and sharing among the entire group to the fullets extent possible. Everyone has an opportunity to express "feelings." In fact, the key to a successful gathering is expressing feelings (rather than trying to impress others with knowledge) and for the group to come to some understanding. The leader can clarify and summarize what has been said, in order to facilitate the group coming to consensus. The leader is often the "Medicine person," with a special understanding of group process based on traditional American Indian training, which is very close to facilitation training.

In earlier years a circle gathering such as the Full Circle gathering was a ceremony for families in conflict, a person seeking his or her purpose in life, or as a "helper" for those who felt that negativity has taken over their lives. Some used it as a clearing-way, or just a yearly ceremony to feel balanced and complete as a person and a family.

As with the Sweat Lodge Ceremony, closed groups provide a necessary continuity to the process. However, it goes without saying that group membership is strictly voluntary. If a person is "referred" to the group the leader provides orientation and sufficiently establishes the interest of the person before he or she actually enters the group. When encountering resistance from a particular member the leader determines whether the participant is not experiencing anything; is experiencing something but does not have the words to express it; or is experiencing something but is not willing to share it. Afterward the appropriate measure can be taken to use the resistance and achieve a better integrated process for that person.

Before we embark on the Full Circle process, it might be helpful for the reader to go through an exercise to lead into the Four Phases, based on the Sweat Lodge Ceremony. One elder called this the "crystal caves to find our healing way."

One must always prepare for a journey. The Full Circle journey is a seven-step process that leads to rebalancing. The person going through the steps will begin with exploring his or her relationship with the world, or *nv wa ti*. The persons's perspective is "laid out on the table to look at," as an elder put it. Just as a journey is planned for, the leader helps the person(s) describe where they are going or what kind of change the person wants with this journey. This is phase I of the journey: Entering.

As it is with any problem-solving or decision-making process, moving through the Four Directions can help to see where a person is in relation to others in a group. A look at the Four Dimensions and asking the questions associated with **belonging, mastery, independence,** and **generosity** can help to clarify what can be worked on to get a truer perspective on where we are and where we are going in our lives. This is phase II of the journey: Crossing the threshold.

Phase III answers some questions by our own vision-seeking and guidance from the leader or Medicine Man and Medicine Woman, as well as spirit guides. At this point we feel somewhat tired of process, or "sweating," and are clarifying where we want to go from here with our lives, our relationships, our spirituality, play and relaxation, work and seeking a new way for ourselves. This is phase III: purifying.

Now we are ready to emerge from this journey of the lodge or the crystal cave for support, review, the "cold plunge," and intervention. This is phase IV: Emergence.

The next chapter will take us through the four phases of the Full Circle Way. This Full Circle Way is a part of the Full Circle gathering. Symbols for this process can be drawn or painted on our Medicine Wheel, which becomes our shield and our guide for renewal or beginning-again with our lives and our relationships.

10
The Four Phases of the Full Circle Way

PHASE I: ENTRANCE

The entrance or beginning phase of the Full Circle process in practice is a time of coming together and "warming up." Members leave everyday settings and influences as they enter the group. Small talk or conversation should be anticipated, as it contributes to group cohesiveness and openness among members. This is a time for members to "test the waters" and reduce anxiety by coming to an understanding of what is appropriate or expected in the group. In this phase participants discuss and establish their rebalancing goals with others.

For the leader, this beginning phase is a time for establishing trust and monitoring verbal and nonverbal communication among members as an initial appraisal of concerns to be explored in the circle. Leaders should be aware that *it's just as important to listen to what people don't say*. The leader's primary goal is to see each of the members as they see themselves—to "step inside their skin," so to speak, in order to get a feel for their worldviews and immediate perspectives.

Entrance into the Full Circle process is characterized by "knowing and letting be known."

PHASE II: THRESHOLD

This part of the Full Circle process is a time for talking about the influences and possible causes of the difficulties being experienced by various members. Investigation is a central component of this stage, the explorations guided by the teachings of the Four Directions. The direct experience of transition unfolds as participants begin to make connections and "see things in a different light."

The trust that is established among members takes on great importance in this phase as each member enters the unknown to receive new knowledge and new understanding. This may be a time of confusion for each of the group members as discrepancies or differences surface concerning self and others. Flexibility and patience are key elements of the leader's role. A rebalancing strategy should be developed by encouraging group members to focus on one of the four directions. Depending upon the concerns and magnitude of disharmony experienced by members, a directive approach may be useful in discovering possibilities and encouraging the group to act as a resource. When someone is coming to the group at the end of a bad day, or something is said in the group that upsets a member or triggers a memory or experience that keeps them from being able to be positive in the group, sometimes it is best to use a more directive approach to have that person express openly what is going through his or her mind. A directive approach, such as using the Talking Stick and saying, "I feel you have something to express. Here is the Talking Stick" gives the person permission to focus on their true feelings.

The threshold phase is ultimately characterized by a culmination in self-understanding.

PHASE III: PURIFICATION

The purification phase of the Full Circle process is a time for choosing a course of action or being that will best lend itself to the restoration of harmony. Each person must choose his or her own harmony. A sense of calm will be evident in group members as rebalancing commences.

It is up to the leader to monitor the level of individual involvement in decision making. The implementation of exercises may prove helpful for members with a clear understanding of their path, as well as for those "outliers" who are still unsure of the best way to attain inner harmony.

A backing up and retracing of previous steps may be necessary for members who require more time to reflect upon what has been learned thus far.

Time should not be regarded as taking precedence over the value of the process, which can proceed at different rates for different people; again, patience is a key factor. It may also be true that a person is not yet ready for harmony. This is an individual decision. The leader's primary responsibility at this point is to open up a world of alternatives and let members decide for themselves the best path to follow. The purification phase is characterized by "choosing."

PHASE IV: EMERGENCE

As a reflection on the process of living, in this final phase of the Full Circle process each member draws together (with the leader's guidance) what she or he has experienced in the group and what has been learned. This is a time for reflection, reaction, and implementation of the choices made for restoring harmony through a rebalancing of the Four Dimensions. During the final sessions members are encouraged to explore the effects of decisions and actions as well as their implications. Possible ways of dealing with implications are discussed. The leader's role becomes one of support, especially through a willingness to explore ramifications with group members.

Emergence is characterized by "doing or letting be done."

THE TALKING CIRCLE

We talk through the circle, and the Circle speaks through us.

The Talking Circle is the physical form that holds the Full Circle explorations. The Talking Circle provides a wonderful opportunity for people to come together. The circle itself becomes a sharing, healing, supportive, and releasing or "giveaway" experience. Traditionally Indian people felt that the circle was a gift by the Great One for healing, as people would come together in nature or in council. The circle was considered to empower people beyond their individual energies. The circle itself is considered by Native Americans as sacred; therefore, coming together into the circle is sacred. The focus of the circle becomes one of harmony and balance.

In a traditional sense one always shows respect for the sacred circle. Aggression is not allowed because that would interfere with the balance of persons in the circle and the harmony of the circle itself. The techniques described in this chapter will focus on the sacredness and purpose of the Talking Circle as a dynamic way that is used at all ages—in meetings, for learning and sharing, for counseling, in community, and for spiritual coming-together activities.

The tone of the circle is first established by a relaxing exercise, prayer, chant with rattle or drum, or music and singing. Verbal expression is less important than the opening of our spirit and inner selves to the greater healing that can take place in the circle. As one Indian elder put it, "It is the shifting from the doing to the being state of oneself that brings about openness and healing." Another Indian elder describes the circle as a "coming together of the past, present, and future" where we sit "in a mode to receive rather than send all the time." The circle becomes a teacher to us as we are more open to the energies around us. Those energies can relax us or enable emotions to flow out of us as we feel protected by the healing of the circle. The circle has a power of its own. If properly used, we can become the recipients of its tremendous healing energy.

A Talking Stick is recommended for guiding the circle experience. The Talking Stick is a special wooden stick with some carvings on it, or with an eagle feather or a crystal attached. Early Cherokees would have used a laurel or sycamore stick, usually seven to twelve inches long, with symbols on it. The significance of the wood had to do with with stories about the first fire and the special wood used for the sacred fire brought to the original people by the Thunder Boys. The symbols on the stick usually represented freedom and protection, as the stick is intended to guide energy.

The Talking Stick is introduced as the Honored One by the group leader, counselor, elder, or Medicine Person.

The Talking Stick is then passed clockwise, with instructions. The circle leader might inquire, for example, "Tell us what you want the circle to know about you," or the instructions may be as simple as "Maybe you have something to share with us as the stick is passed to you." A person's identity is less important than the thoughts or feelings she or he would like to share. Group members should be told that this is a good time to let down one's mask and be open to expressing the inner self within the protected and respected environment of the circle. (With this level of sharing it is easy to see how the interference of people coming in and out of the circle can be uncomfortable for participants. Therefore, permission should be requested of the group before entering or leaving the circle.) The circle leader observes the subtle expressions of members in the circle, directing participants to either release pain and emotions or exhibit self-control as the circle "feels" its way along the path of healing. The leader can also gauge when the circle needs to become a Healing Circle.

A trained Medicine Person knows how to be the gatekeeper for energy flow and focus in the circle. It takes some experience to guide a circle, particularly for healing or shifting the circle's energy flow. For example, suppose that a member of the circle becomes overwhelmed with emotion; a Medicine Person may go over to the participant and open his or her arms as a gesture of support. The Talking Circle can easily become a Healing Circle to focus on the experience of pain or loss of one or more persons. It could also be helpful for working through emotional subjects such as coping with AIDS or some traumatic conflict. The circle leader, if not a trained counselor or Medicine Person, may want to have such a person in the group. The circle may also have "helpers," members who facilitate the healing process or provide support during an opportunity for healing. These helpers may be intentionally present, or they may emerge as the situation arises. Many kinds of helpers that traditionally used by Native American people with the circle. These included the fire; certain minerals, herbs, and teas; feathers; and many other objects. Today the most common helpers are the Talking Stick or eagle feather. These helpers are considered to guide and support as they become part of the healing process. As an elder put it, "Let the helper help, not hinder the healing process." Having an object such as the Talking Stick give permission for openness to healing is very powerful. The same elder also said, "The helper [object] is a power that connects our energy with the universal energy."

Sometimes in the course of the Full Circle way it is important to convene a Healing Circle as a helper in facilitating a member's healing process. The group becomes a circle of healing energy that provides harmony and balance to a "dis-eased" person. The focus is on energy rather than activity. In a Healing Circle the emphasis is on relaxation and receptivity for the facilitation of healing. As an Indian elder put it, "Healing is something that is rather than something you make happen. The healing energy is already there, or it comes from the Universal Circle." The key is to shut down your own energy by focusing on music, prayer, or chants, or by using visualizations that allow you to act as a conduit for the flow of energy to the person in need of the Good Medicine energy. With a little practice the group becomes as one, a unified "energy pool," so to speak, upon which participants can draw.

A wonderful exercise with the hands can aid in learning about energy. Try putting your hands together, finger-to-finger and palms touching. Experience the wonderful calm in raising the hands at a comfortable level in front of you, then feel the energy rush as you allow the hands to slowly drop downward without touching your legs. In the circle, practice holding hands (upon getting permission from the participants) and then feel what happens when the hands drop apart from one another. The ideal situation is to have a well-balanced group, standing with hands at your side in calm relaxation.

We are connected to the Great One from the beginning of the
fire of life to the beginning-again.

Then grab each other's hands comfortably, with permission. The energy rush feels very reassuring. To feel the difference, try joining hands after visualizing or talking about something that is upsetting to the group. The up-and-down surges can seem interfering or make you feel anxious about trying to achieve calm. This demonstrates the importance of feeling inner calm before working with healing energy.

The Healing Circle can practice moving the energy around the circle by directing the flow verbally and visualizing its movement in a particular direction. The energy tends to pull or tug, causing some movement in the individual and the whole circle. Direct the flow in the opposite direction and then feel the shift of the energy flow. Once this is done, work on relaxing with the energy at a calm state.

Another exercise is to sit or stand in the circle and direct energy to come into the circle from the Universal Circle, which can occur around the fire, as was done by Indians in earlier years for ceremony and healing. It takes some practice to accomplish even receptivity by all in the group, primarily because different people are on different levels of learning. The idea is to visualize energy coming into each person in the group for healing and wellness. The elder Indian teachers say that prayer chants or some way of protecting the individual and group is needed before bringing energy inside the circle. The best way is to have the group, sitting on blankets on Mother Earth, visualize sending their negative energy (or energy that needs to be cleared) into Mother Earth. Then the group can draw or fill energy from the universal energy of the Sun or even the sky. The idea is to avoid negative or interfering energy influences around us.

As a Cherokee elder once said, "It is best to learn these

[energy] exercises using a guide or Medicine teacher so that only Good Medicine is there with you." The location where you or the group works with energy is very important. Persons who are trained understand the negative influences and can pick the locations and even the spots in the circle best suited for each person. As the members become proficient in handling energy, the group develops into a Healing Circle.

The purpose of the Healing Circle in this instance is to be a helper in facilitating the healing process. The process itself takes place within each individual; a person in need of a Healing Circle is most often unable to focus under the "dis-eased" situation. The intent is to provide healing support to anyone in need, but the Healing Circle should not replace any practitioner methodology or approach being used by the individual as physical or mental treatment. The intent is to facilitate harmony and balance. This is an educational facilitation, not a medical approach or treatment. With this in mind, the Healing Circle is an exciting experience that can initiate beautiful results in the form of harmony and balance, bringing the person and the group into Full Circle.

A Cherokee elder said, "The circle has no beginning or end, but everyone is in the middle with everyone else. We are not alone in the circle, and we are connected—one to another."

11
Techniques and Exercises

Calm is healing.

Many of the techniques used in the Full Circle process have application in our lives outside the rebalancing circle. As an elder put it, "We have become so mechanized in our daily lives that we have forgotten much about feeling and using our intuitive self. The way to get back to that feeling and healing is to get back to nature." A mother in a Full Circle group said, "Children have become experts at playing on computers, but they don't know how to play outside anymore."

The techniques and exercises in this chapter are based on traditional Native American teachings and ceremonies. They open our feeling self and allow us to play. Many of the traditional techniques and exercises are for individual as well as group application.

The healing circle discussed earlier is used in every Full Circle gathering, either for individual benefit or as a group technique. Often it is not identified as such; it involves a song or prayer-chant with drumming. We also use what we call "Inner Circles." Full Circle participants sit or stand in a large circle, while the Inner Circle is focused on a teaching, such as using the crystals or an eagle feather for "healing energy" work. The Inner Circle may be a teaching on most any subject, but a traditional story is used to tie the lesson to a traditional way.

Oftentimes the groups will be divided into Four Directions as clans, such as the Bear Clan from the West or the Deer Clan from the North. Each will be given an exercise that they will learn themselves and teach the entire group.

The techniques and exercises can be age-related to have full participation of everyone in the Full Circle gathering. It is understood that every technique and exercise is in some way focused on healing, even if it is to just relax the spirit. An Inner Circle for "healing the spirit" is used in small groups with no more than three persons in the Inner Circle. The Medicine Man or elder uses a crystal or eagle feather as traditionally trained, as well as using a rattle with a prayer-chant or using the drumming to relax the persons in the Inner Circle. Of course, the outer circle is relaxing as well.

Sometimes a circle inside the larger circle will be used for energy movement using different techniques of "energy work." Also, as an elder put it, "Anyone can experience the healing energy of nature by just sitting beneath a tree where they are comfortable and protected." The person uses deep breathing, then asks that healing energy come from Mother Earth, the tree, and the inner circle of the environment. With practice, one can learn to direct the energy for localized healing.

These techniques have been used by American Indians and other cultures throughout the world since the beginning of time. Is it actual healing occurring or is it the training of focusing chemical and energy action internally? An elder responds, "What difference does it make as long as it works. It matters that people are involved in the process and the choice for healing."

The techniques and exercises to follow are to be used as

activities for the larger group gathering in the circle, as well as Inner Circle teachings for healing, harmony, and balance.

SHARING OF A MEAL

In earlier years everyone in the tribe, clan, or gathering of families would be included in preparing the meal. The elders would be served by the young ones. The adults would take care of the "little ones" who were below the age of seven by having certain adults assigned to play games with them. Some would be practicing a prayer or a song to share with the meal. Everyone participated: even the smallest would be doing something to learn about the task of preparing a meal, feast, or a ceremony. It was a family-centered activity for all ages.

In the Full Circle gathering, people bring things to share with the group, such as natural snack foods and teas, which becomes a gesture of acceptance and gifting among the group. The sharing of food demonstrates respect for life, as people begin to relax and to help "let their guard down," so to speak. It also represent a coming-together for sharing, caring, honoring an occasion or person(s), and just feeling good or healing.

THE TALKING CIRCLE

As mentioned earlier, the Talking Circle is central to Full Circle healing. This practice traditionally serves as a forum for the expression of thoughts and feelings in a context of complete acceptance by group members.

Step 1: Participants form a circle together. A traditional chant with music, rattle, or drumming may be used for relaxation and clearing as people enter the circle. When everyone has gathered initial greetings are made. The crystal, eagle feather, or Talking Stick is used in the group as a sacred object representing truth and understanding as powerful agents of healing. The Medicine object, as it is sometimes called by way of whoever holds it, signifies permission to speak.

The leader begins by picking up the Talking Stick to share feelings or concerns with the group. When the leader has spoken, the Talking Stick is passed clockwise to the next person, who may speak or choose to remain silent. Again, the Talking Stick is passed to the next person.

Step 2: During the circle gathering questions may be asked with verbal exchanges taking place, but only by permission of whoever is holding the stick. Another member wishing to speak about something not related to what the "stick holder" is discussing must wait her turn. The leader, too, should feel free to ask questions or make clarifying statements, but again, only by permission of the one who holds the stick.

Step 3: When the Talking Stick has made at least two or three rounds, having been passed to all participants, it is laid in the center of the circle to be picked up by anyone wishing to speak further. When all those who want to speak are finished, the Talking Circle can be brought to a close with a traditional chant or blessing-way to give thanks for the coming-together. It is understood that what was said in the circle remains in the circle to demonstrate respect for all members and to protect the sacredness of the occasion.

TECHNIQUES FOR PHASE I: ENTERING

Time-perspective

Time-perspective is an assessment technique whose application in itself is healing. Time-perspective provides the helper with information on an individual's level of functioning by revealing some very important facets of that person's worldview and immediate perspective. Mutual understanding is the primary goal of Time-perspective. In addition, it can be used as a springboard for discussion and for defining what discrepancies a person is experiencing, or specifically what she or he wants to work on.

Full Circle draws on a person's level of functioning based on (1) the knowledge of self that comes from past experiences and ways of coping; (2) the present view of self and understanding of possible discrepancies being experienced; and (3) the goals and purposes that person is working toward in the future. These three components of a person's life are interrelated and interfunctioning; for example, knowledge of self from past experiences feeds into the present view of self, which in turn influences that person's goals and sense of purpose, which cycle back around to guide a person's perceptions of experiences and knowledge of self, and so on and so forth. These three levels essentially run "full circle." Hence, Time-perspective "slices" Full Circle into three time-related realms:

1. Knowing (self-awareness) represents past functioning;

2. Being (the Inner Circle) represents present functioning; and

3. Doing (life purpose) represents future functioning.

The questioning sequence provides a means for establishing rapport in a nonthreatening way by exploring these three realms. In this way, Time-perspective is used to increase self-awareness and to promote a deeper understanding of the Full Circle healing process. The following questions can be used to identify the discrepancies a person is experiencing and to discuss key issues from the past, present, and future.

Past

1. What is one of the best things that has ever happened to you? Describe it.

2. What did you learn from that experience? What did you take away from it? What stands out for you from that experience?

Present

3. How do you see yourself now after having gone through that experience?

4. What do you really live for? What makes life worth living for you?

5. What are the main discrepancies or conflicts in your life now?

6. How would life be different if you didn't have this discrepancy?

7. What is working for you right now? What is working against you?

Future

8. What do you think the future holds for you?

9. What is something you are looking forward to? What are you working toward?

Rebalancing Technique

The entire Full Circle gathering is about rebalancing, while a person's entire life is about keeping themselves in balance. The key to this technique is to have choice in everything going on in the larger outer circle and in the Inner Circle teachings. For example, sometimes a person just wants to watch and that is all right. (Staying present is important as part of the participation, rather than leaving the circle.) Rebalancing is also a way to ensure that everyone is interacting in some way. "Helpers" are assigned to observe what is going on with everyone so that interaction, emotion, attentiveness, and feelings are protected while participation is maximized. As an elder put it, "the most athletic youth is not necessarily the best athlete. A team working together with all its skills and talents becomes the best. The same is true with games of telling stories and ceremonial activities. It is not the individual but the performance of the group that we focus on, while the helpers guide the results."

In rebalancing we focus on what a person is doing right or what is going on in that person's life that is positive and reassuring for them. For example, a healing circle may focus on an activity for "feeling good" such as planting a tree and watching it grow. The joy an elder or a little one can get from measuring its growth each year after the cold season is a positive and reaffirming activity of life. If it dies, we know about it, and the group is there with two trees to plant the next year. As an elder said, "Listening well is one of the little things that counts."

TECHNIQUES FOR PHASE II: CROSSING THE THRESHOLD

The Four Directions

While we have discussed the Four Directions throughout this book, it is easier for those who have not experienced a Full Circle gathering or a traditional ceremony to picture a group of about fifty to seventy people sitting in a large circle inside a room, or sitting outside on blankets or chairs. This is the larger outer group. Full Circle always starts with a blessing of the drum, which is about two feet in diameter with four or more drummers using a two-step, four-time beat. An entry song is sung while participants enter the room, after being smudged with sage and cedar. Smudging is a smoke from the burning plants that is moved quickly around you as you enter the room; it is a traditional form of clearing.

When we are all seated the leader initiates with a traditional prayer-chant or song-chant in Cherokee. This is followed by soft flute playing to help the group relax and "come-together in energy and spirit." As an elder says, " We call upon our ancestors to be with us as we come together in the circle of friends. We give thanks to the Great One for this day."

> **Step 1:** All of the members sit together in a circle. An explanation of the Four Directions is given to the group by the leader, with descriptions of strengths and some examples of what each Direction represents concerning personal development.

Step 2: In order to better orient everyone to the Four Directions, use a compass to determine the location of each of the directions. To ensure familiarity, have a few members identify the following about themselves for the group:

> **East:** Something that is changing your life toward becoming more at one with yourself, others, and your surroundings or circumstances.

> **South:** Something you have recently found that brings out the child in you; something that is fun or enjoyable for you.

> **West:** An activity or way of doing things for increasing your own self-awareness that has helped you or can help you improve your life.

> **North:** A way or a place you can find inner calm and relaxation that allows you to get in touch with yourself; what wisdom is gained and how you can offer it to others.

This process will allow each of the members to get acquainted with the Four Directions and with themselves. Sharing of why a particular direction was chosen and what came to mind is important for gathering reactions and any intuitive insights received.

Step 3: Continue by identifying each of the Four Directions again. Each person is then asked to choose a direction in which they feel that they symbolically are at present. This can be done silently, or by having the group members actually get up and move to the designated direction that they have chosen after coming together in the center.

Time is given for members of the same direction to talk among themselves, and later for those who wish to share with the group reasons for them being in this particular direction and their feelings about it. It is important to realize that there may be some who do not know or may sense themselves as being in more than one direction. These are people who are likely in some transition; this should be explained to them in positive terms as an opportunity to select one direction only, then discuss feelings in the group selected. The leader can also decide one direction for the person in order to move the process forward and to avoid encouraging conflict in the decisions made by others.

Step 4: Encourage the members in each of the respective directions to answer the following questions concerning the Four Dimensions:

> **Belonging** is characterized by the presence of trust and caring in relations with others: *Who or what are you a part of?*

> **Mastery** is manifested by a recognition of abilities and a person's sense of meaningful achievement in his or her life: *What do you enjoy doing well?*

> **Independence** represents a belief in oneself through the presence of self-awareness and self-discipline: *What do you believe in?* or *What is important to you?*

Generosity is characterized by an openness to experience represented by the ability for trust and sharing: *What do you have to share?*

Step 5: Everyone comes together once again in the center of the circle. Each member now selects a direction where they would like to be in the future. Again, the leader may choose to have the participants get up and move to that direction. Plenty of time should be given for members to reflect and discuss their situations. For those who wish to share with the group, "talking" time will provide a forum to work through certain discrepancies in their lives.

The center of the circle should be discussed as representing balance among all Four Directions. Acknowledge that every person has his or her own unique center that may fall at different places within the circle. Possible ways of understanding and dealing with discrepancies can be discussed. Remind participants that all Four Dimensions are necessary for wellness through harmony and balance.

Transitioning

The technique of Transitioning lends an in-depth understanding of the source and extent of imbalance. Drawing on a particular period of transition that a person has experienced, it identifies ways of coping and views of self that may be helpful in dealing with a present situation or discrepancy. By clarifying a past experience and the course of action or reaction taken, a person has the opportunity to draw parallels (connections) and recognize patterns (separation) of thought, feeling, or behavior as well as resources for dealing with difficult experiences.

A series of questions helps to clarify what is at the heart of a perceived imbalance. Such questions follow.

1. What is one of the toughest things you've ever had to face? Can you remember a time when you experienced a major transition?

2. What happened? What was going on?

3. What did you do? How did you get through it? How did you deal with it?

4. How long did it take to overcome this difficulty?

5. How did your feelings change through it all?

6. How are you different now as a result of going through that experience? What did you learn about yourself from that experience?

7. Can you think of anything you did then that could be helpful to you now? Could you use anything from that experience to help you now?

The questioning sequence systematically takes a person through any transition experience specifically identifying what was going on, what was being experienced, what was done, and what the consequences were. These experiences are significant resources to draw upon for the process of change. Increased self-awareness, clarification of life-purpose, and deepened understanding of present discrepancies are but a few of the benefits gained from the Transitioning exercise. It provides an opportunity for clarifying purpose and direction of change.

Natural Consequences

The Natural Consequences technique is used in conjunction with Transitioning as a way of achieving a deeper understanding of the source and extent of imbalance. Whereas Transitioning seeks parallels between past experiences and present ones, Natural Consequences draws on a person's learning through the integration of new experiences, both in the past and present, and the dissolution of unuseful expectations for the future. In this way self-awareness is increased, life-purpose may be further clarified, and discrepancies are further understood and dealt with by exploring the consequences of change.

Every decision can have both "good" and "bad" effects. Natural Consequences uses an in-depth description by either the participant or the helper to identify what the desirable and undesirable consequences would be if the discrepancy were eliminated. Traditionally this exercise would be used to teach skills of hunting or plants for Medicine. Natural consequences would be such things as planting the seeds at a time when they would not germinate, or not being quiet long enough for the deer to come close enough to pierce with an arrow. The word *discrepancy* denoted what you would do again for a successful outcome. The same could be true of meeting a young girl for the first time and saying the "right" things.

The lesson to learn is that we must make things right when we do things wrong or create a dishonorable act for our family. For young people, this is a way to help teach values of being responsible for their actions so as to not embarrass the family, clan, or tribe. As an elder said, "We are recognized as Indian because we are a member of a tribe. We also recognize that we must always be and act responsibly so as not to bring harm to the tribe or our family because of our actions." This is also a technique to look at what we did or could do "wrong" and how to make things "right."

The following list of questions can be used to incite discussion between the participant and the leader or helper(s).

1. How would things be different if you didn't have this discrepancy?

2. If you could be the way you wanted, how would you be? What would that consist of specifically?

3. What are all of the "negative" consequences that could occur if you eliminated this discrepancy?

4. What's the worst that could happen?

5. What would happen if you didn't do anything to make things better?

6. What would that mean to you or the other person?

7. What would that be saying to you about yourself?

While asking the above questions, particular attention should be given to the "negative" consequences, as these restraining factors can be strategically reframed to be more desirable but challenging. For instance, if a person were to give up being depressed he would be able to make friends, which could be stressful and may lead to rejection.

Hence, the participant has an opportunity to actually take a look at and deal with some of the anticipated "drawbacks" of change. Essentially, the Natural Consequences exercise makes the known or unknown more tangible; it can then be reframed as a challenge to be conquered rather than feared.

Ambivalence or restraint thus becomes a means to change instead of a barrier.

TECHNIQUES FOR PHASE III: PURIFYING

Sourcing

This is one of the primary techniques used in the process of rebalancing. In earlier years "sourcing," or "getting to the bottom of the fears" as an elder called it, was a way to help young people and adults not be afraid of the dark in going through the woods, or dealing with negative reactions or actions as a result of a dog bite or a frightening experience. While those are simple examples, more complex situations can occur from abuse and anxiety reaction today.

Sourcing is based on the notion that our actions and reactions (thoughts, feelings, behaviors) serve some important purposes for us, whether constructive or destructive, and that the need for such a "purposeful" response has its source in our innermost fears or uncertainties.

Many of the things we do or the ways we react have their origins in our fears. Looking at our actions and reactions in terms of the functions they perform leads to a better understanding of some the emotional choices we make on a daily basis.

The following list of questions can be used as a guide for understanding the source of a participant's thoughts, feelings, and behavior.

1. What happens when you experience a thought, feeling or behavior that feels frightening or causes you some anxiety?

2. Can you give me some specific examples?

3. What are you saying to yourself when that happens?

4. What does this (thought, feeling, or behavior) say to you about yourself?

5. When does it happen? How often? Under what circumstances?

6. Hypothetically, what's the worst that could happen?

7. What makes you afraid of that? What do you see yourself as having to lose?

8. What purpose or function do you think your thought, feeling, or behavior serves for you? In what way is it useful for you?

9. Where does this way of thinking, feeling or behaving come from?

10. How do you think it came about for you?

Considering the source of these decisions allows for different choices to be made, if that is what a person wants. Our intentions are a very important part of the consequences we experience both within ourselves and between ourselves and others.

Sourcing leads to increased self-awareness, allowing for a deeper understanding of the fears or uncertainties guiding our choices and thereby helping us develop an attitude toward living based on courage rather than avoidance or deflection. With this practice discrepancies can be dealt with in a more constructive way through the simultaneous use of other techniques appropriate to the rebalancing process.

Reframing

Based on the lesson taught to us by the Rule of Opposites, Reframing uses perspective as an invaluable tool in the process of understanding and change. Reframing is an old technique used by American Indians to put things in perspective. The elders are very good at "framing" things for meaning and purpose, as well as "reframing" things to bring about meaning that is useful to us.

Once a young boy cried because he did not shoot the rabbit like his father pierced the deer for supper. An elder said, "Youngdeer, what happened?"

The boy sobbed and said, "I tried to track the rabbit as my father taught me, and I was close, but the arrow slipped, and I missed. My dad is going to be mad at me."

The elder said, "You missed the rabbit, or did the rabbit miss your arrow? Maybe it was not his time to be dinner." In reframing the elder asked, "Will your dad be mad at you, or will he be glad that you are learning your skills? Maybe you are mad at yourself, because you are not bringing home a rabbit to make your dad proud of you. I know he is already proud of you, because you are learning to be a good hunter." In finishing the elder asked the boy, "Did you thank the rabbit for this opportunity to practice your skills as a hunter?"

In the Full Circle gatherings we use "reframing" a lot to clarify what people really mean, or ask participants to reframe statements in a positive way for making things better, rather than making them feeling worse.

The technique results in a new perspective to view oneself, others, or situations. The following excerpt taken Viktor Frankl's *Psychotherapy and Existentialism* (1967) illustrates the powerful impact Reframing can have on an individual's point of reference.

> Once, an elderly general practitioner consulted me because of his severe depression. He could not overcome the loss of his wife who had died two years before and whom he had loved above all else. Now how could I help him? What should I tell him? Well, I refrained from telling him anything, but instead confronted him with the question, "What would have happened, Doctor, if you had died first, and your wife would have had to survive you?" "Oh," he said, "for her this would have been terrible; how she would have suffered!" Whereupon I replied, "You see, Doctor, such a suffering has been spared her, and it is you who have spared her this suffering; but now, you have to pay for it by surviving and mourning her." He said no word but shook my hand and calmly left my office. Suffering ceases to be suffering in some way at the moment it finds a meaning, such as the meaning of a sacrifice.

Reframing consists of changing the participant's frame of reference by introducing a slightly different meaning than that attributed to a situation. Some inquiries that help to facilitate Reframing include:

What if . . . ?

Could it be that . . . ?

Have you ever thought about . . . ?

Is it possible . . . ?

Maybe . . . ?

What would it mean if . . . ?

Reframing can make constructive use of defeating perceptions or beliefs about oneself, others, or situations rather than attempting to counter them or eliminate them through coercion. For example, one can change "I [do this] because [this happens]" to "*When* I [do this], [this happens]." Ultimately, perceptions of choice affect choices made. Reframing is a mildly confrontational way of offering alternative ways of perceiving things mixed with a subtle invitation for the person to choose the best or most useful way of looking at those things.

PURIFICATION TECHNIQUES OF THE EAST: BELONGING

Each Direction has its own purification way that emphasizes the values of that direction. The East focuses on belonging to the family, clan, and tribe as a member who shares and contributes to the "good Medicine," as an elder put it. Sometimes it is important to understand confrontation with members who try to take charge, rather than accept humility as their strength.

There are some fun techniques in the East Direction that can help us learn to get along and enjoy each other's company. The first technique, "I-Me," can be confrontational, but guiding and clarifying. "Switching" is another way of saying, "put yourself in my shoes." The Friendship Circle brings people together in an enjoyable activity.

The I–Me Technique

The I–Me technique is used to redirect a person's attention from looking inside-out to looking outside-in. A more objective evaluation of reactions and feelings can be achieved by a person who is encouraged to "step outside of their skin" every

once in a while. This is especially helpful for those who become so entrenched in habitual ways of reacting that they no
longer think clearly or make good personal decisions for
wellness.

Two young Native American boys, as the story goes, were
always very competitive through their younger years in learning how to survive under the leadership of their grandfather.
Their own father lost his life during the Civil War. Guiding
the two boys was a difficult task for the elder, particularly as
he saw Jim nih become too competitive and resentful of his
brother Mi kih. Jim and Mike, as they were called in English,
farmed a small plot of land provided by the grandfather. Jim
tended to find shortcuts so he could spend more time at the
waterhole playing with the other young people. He did not
like to pull the weeds or "hoe up the rows," especially when it
meant getting up early or working late in the afternoon. Mike
worked hard in the small plot of land and liked to share the
Indian corn they planted with others.

Jim said, "You are a fool to share, because we can trade it for
nice things at the opening of the Green Corn Ceremony." Mike
did not respond, but knew that sharing brought honor to the
family. "I am going to have the best-looking Indian corn so the
young girls will notice me at festival time," said Jim. Mike said
nothing, knowing that his brother really missed the attention
of their late father. Mike could feel his hurt, but knew that his
dad would be proud of a well-kept farming plot, as he continued to hoe and build the mounds around the corn stalks.

Late in the afternoon one day, a sudden storm came over
the mountains with very dark clouds and bursts of thunder
as the Thunder Beings were playing Indian ball in the sky field.
The rain started to pour very hard. Jim was nowhere to be

found, so Mike took his wooden hoe stick to shore the stalks. He saw the corn stalks in Jim's plot being blown down by the wind and rain. He quickly shored the rows in Jim's plot with his hoe, but only completed about three of the seven rows before the rain came down in buckets, so to speak.

After the storm, Jim and Mike stood looking at the damage done by the wind and rain. Four rows of Jim's plot were totally destroyed and corn stalks from both plots were bent over from the rain and wind. It was painfully obvious that Jim was left with only the three rows that his brother had saved during the storm. Although he was sad, Jim thanked his brother and the Great One for the painful lesson learned. "I was the foolish one," said Jim, looking in Mike's direction. "While it hurts me inside, I know that I need to follow my feeling and the teachings of our grandfather. Our father would want it that way."

In this story, the "I" becomes a projection of not listening to the "Me" as selfishness overcomes judgment based on the teachings and feelings of the person. While both are a part of us, traditional Indian teachings reflect that "I" sometimes misleads us, acting out from the "Me" that attempts to maintain inner harmony and balance. The "I" is impulsive and child-like in its demands for attention, while the "Me" provides reason and self-control.

The use of the "I–Me" dynamic is a good way to have an individual or group of individuals observe their reactions and the interaction of both components in their lives. In the circle setting, a variety of issues can be focused on using the "I" reaction within the group, then asking for the "Me" reaction, feeling, or thoughts. A little practice can result in a coming-together of the two, allowing the group and individual persons to focus on gaps in reactions. The purpose is to talk through the gaps and to crystallize the reactions toward harmony and balance. Understanding the "I–Me" dynamic can also be very useful as a "reality test" to clarify what we really think and to discuss why we react or think in a certain way. The result often provides an opportunity to choose the feelings and thoughts you want the "I" to express as a reflection of your new or renewed path.

The I–Me technique is especially helpful for diffusing intense emotional states and for recognizing true reactions beyond simple defensive responses. In addition, it is an excellent means of helping members to understand and own their reactions in a way that encourages better choices for wellness.

Step 1: A participant is selected by the leader to communicate with the leader, since this technique works on an individual basis. The person is asked to describe a particular disturbing or uncomfortable situation, and his or her reactions and feelings about that situation.

Step 2: Once the concern(s) are identified, the leader establishes the "I" component by enlisting a feeling of frustration or anger paired with an "I am" statement. For example, a participant's "I" component may be expressed as "I'm really angry that people ignore me."

Step 3: The leader then works on establishing the "Me" component by reversing the situation and asks the following questions:

1. "How would you feel if I were the one with this conflict instead of you?"

2. "What are some helpful things you might suggest to me? What words of advice might you offer me for dealing with my conflict?"

For instance, following the example from above the leader may ask, "How would you feel if I were the one being ignored instead of you?" This provides an opportunity for the participant to reflect on his or her concern from a different perspective. Essentially the participant is asked to look at others in the same situation and examine how they react. The contrast may not initially be evident to the participant, who will tend to cling to the "I" as a way of dealing with concerns. However, as the leader progressively brings the hypothetical situation onto a more believable personal level, some insight may be received by the participant. Appropriate self-disclosure on the part of the leader could prove useful.

Switching

The Switching technique is especially useful for those experiencing some sort of conflict or discrepancy with another person, such as a friend, associate, or family member. Switching is a spin-off of Sourcing, applied to interpersonal difficulties that result in discrepancy.

The following questioning sequence for Switching explores different perspectives, functions, and sources of the actions or reactions of others.

1. What is this person doing that bothers you?

2. Let's say you were in the same situation as this person, what are some possible reasons you would be doing or saying that?

3. What do you think this person is saying to him- or herself when that happens?

4. What do you think this individual would say if asked why she or he is doing that?

5. What purposes might this particular behavior serve for him or her? In what way is this behavior useful for this individual?

6. Where do you think this behavior might have come from? How do you think it came about for this person?

7. In what ways was your situation different from this one? How is it similar?

Afterward the participant assumes the role of that other person and attempts to convincingly represent his or her point of view with conviction; the leader plays "devil's advocate" by assuming the participant's point of view. Any number of insights into another's behavior may result from the methodical use of perspective. This technique also encourages a certain level of open-mindedness in the participant by virtue of taking part in the process. By having the participant switch roles, both through the questioning sequence and role-playing, discrepancies can be better understood and thereby dealt with in a more effective way.

The Friendship Circle (Dance)

The Friendship Circle is especially fun and effective with children and the child inside of us as adults. It evokes the memory of children holding hands, laughing, and dancing in circles. Its purpose is to reinforce friendship in the circle. Depending on age and the tempo of the music or the traditional chants used, the rattle or drum can determine how quickly the circle goes around. The circle can go in either direction, but at a certain point the leader or "head person" drops hands with one person in the circle and leads into the Inner Circle, going around until the circle is bunched up into the Friendship Circle.

To better picture the movement with the drumming, imagine that everyone is in a circle moving around with a two-step or a slide shuffle. The "Head Dancer" enters the circle to move the participants inside of the circle, going around until they cannot move anymore, then the drumming stops. Everybody yells, "Ah hoh!"

Another use of the Friendship Circle is to get a group together and slowly move using a shuffle or slide by holding hands and going around or dropping hands and following the "head person" around into the circle. The focus is to have relaxing fun and to treat the circle as sacred, similar to the traditional dances around the fire in earlier years.

The Friendship Circle can be used with all ages by focusing on a particular subject, such as clearing the mind and spirit or giving thanks. It can also be a good way of ending a long group session or facilitating some activity, workshop, or meeting to reinforce the "coming-together" of people in friendship.

PURIFICATION TECHNIQUES OF
THE SOUTH: MASTERY

The purification ways of the South include "Mirroring," which is a way of looking at ourselves by having someone else mirror back to us. "Crazy Dog Technique" is not used that much today, but it is a form of critical review as well as being a helper to others to see that there is choice in all things "except death and taxes." Crazy Dog might explore ways there is choice in taxes, or even in death, understanding that absolutes can sometimes be harmful. Therefore, the opposite is proposed to at least think about and to discuss in an Inner Circle.

Another technique is the "Split-Self," which allows the leader to assume what a person is feeling. The purpose is to help the person feel better about how they feel and to make something positive out of that feeling. "River Rock" is a wonderful technique for children and adults alike. By carrying something around that is a reminder of a problem or issue, it is easier to let it go or skip it across the water or just bury it in Mother Earth as a clearing-way.

Mirroring

Mirroring is essentially a way of restating a person's position by accepting it as being unconditionally true or emulating the same position. This can be in the form of words or in actions. Exaggeration can be used to help a person see what she or he is really saying or doing and how those things are perceived by others. Awareness and understanding are two goals of the Mirroring exercise.

Thus, Mirroring involves accepting and exaggerating the participant's position by playing the "game of opposites." A helper is expected to help or "fix what's broken." But what if the helper assists by not trying to help in the way that is expected? Instead of trying to convince, educate, or argue the participant out of his or her frame of reference, in the Mirroring exercise the leader simply takes the same position and exaggerates it by "going the participant one-better."

Oftentimes a leader will introduce some teaching points

and a helper will guide the group. Usually the helper is chosen among the group to ask the questions to the leader, or to be the facilitator of the group. Traditionally this technique was a way to have something mirrored back to the person so he or she can understand how it feels to someone else. Usually whatever the person says in frustration or response is repeated back, like this: "I don't agree with you!"

"You don't agree with me?"

"I already said that I don't agree with you! How does it feel for me to not agree with you?"

"Frankly, it ticks me off!"

"Do you want to reframe this discussion so it's not about agreement or disagreement and is about how you feel?"

Sometimes a "cool off" period is suggested and then the person is asked to come back and reframe it. Other times mirroring it back provides an opportunity for the person to admit that they did not mean it like that, and they go on to explain. Actually, this happens often with people who may want to get their point across, or make sure they are heard. Traditionally mirroring is used with children, for them to see how they are acting, and with adults who were not humble or respectful in a group. It is also used as a way to clarify.

The Crazy Dog Technique

The Crazy Dog technique is a direct descendant of the traditions practiced by the Contrary Society. Borrowing from the Rule of Opposites and the notion that for every choice there is a non-choice or alternative that is just as applicable, the Crazy Dog technique draws upon opposites in order to release a person from habitual ways of acting or reacting. The goal is shifting a person away from a self-defeating, one-directional approach to a two-directional approach that recognizes the function of actions or reactions.

In Full Circle, a Crazy Dog Inner Circle can be chosen with three participants; they will remind us of the opposite way of thinking while we are in another teaching Inner Circle. In one of our Full Circle gatherings we used this kind of an Inner Circle to look at an issue involving the drilling of oil wells in the Alaska tundra, which created lots of discussion as a pro and con activity. It was a way for us to reframe the issue and look for alternatives as an exercise in clan groups.

People often get locked into acting certain ways and to reacting in a limited manner. Sometimes this one-way path stifles perceptions of choice, resulting in feelings of helplessness or ambivalence. The Crazy Dog technique explores the consequences of opposite actions or reactions by encouraging participants to reverse normal expectations for behavior by doing the opposite or reacting in the opposite way than would normally be expected. The following questioning sequence can be used to facilitate this technique:

1. What would it *feel like* if you were to act, feel or think just the opposite of what you do now or what you are expected to do?

2. What would *happen* if you acted, felt or thought just the opposite of what you do now or what you are supposed to do?

Here it is important not that the participant doesn't feel what you're asking her to, but that she attempts to do so. Sincerity is not the key; what's important is that a sincere attempt is made. Participants may be astonished to observe how others respond to their changed behavior as well as how they respond to themselves. This technique often results in the discovery of an extremely useful new talent: choice.

Split-Self Technique

This is a role-playing technique that "splits" the participant into two parts. The leader assumes the participant's role as "person" and tries to "be" him or her. Meanwhile, the participant assumes the role of a voice (that is, conscience) whose job it is to convince the "person" of the opposite. The "person" (or leader playing the participant) starts by making a statement or series of statements similar to those previously expressed in the circle gathering. The voice (or participant) must then attempt to convince the person that the opposite is true and give specific reasons why, taken from his or her life.

This exchange might proceed in the following way:

Person: I'm kind of lonely. And it's obvious that nobody really cares for me. . . .

Voice: But you're a good person, you know. And you've got lots of friends and people who think pretty well of you.

Person: Like who?

Voice: Well, there's _____, and_____ . . . .

Person: But they don't call me very much, and when I call them it seems like they just don't have the time for me.

Voice: Maybe they don't have the time or maybe you call at bad times. You know, people do have a lot of things going on in their lives, but that doesn't necessarily mean that they don't care for you.

In this way participants are forced into countering their own statements. In facing some of their own thoughts and feelings, individuals gain a better understanding of the role they play in the discrepancy being experienced. Moreover, ways of dealing with self-defeating thoughts, feelings, and behaviors can be discussed and practiced for making better choices.

The River Rock Technique

The process of living always involves something to learn, something to experience, something to understand. There are both "good" experiences and "bad" ones, depending on individual interpretation. What we take away from each experience varies from situation to situation and from time to time and is simply a question of choice. Unfortunately, we sometimes get so caught up in troubling experiences and the destructive feelings and thoughts therein that we are essentially unable to experience the satisfying ones. In a sense, we do not allow ourselves to experience the good experiences until we are ready, until we decide that whatever burden we are carrying is no longer worth the weight.

> **Step 1:** The River Rock technique involves asking someone to choose a river rock of appropriate size and weight for each of their "problems." These are to be self-induced problems that could easily be done away with, like dropping one's river rocks when one becomes tired of carrying or maintaining them. Remind the person that healing is a serious process, and therefore the task at hand should be taken just as seriously.

> **Step 2:** Ask the person to carry the river rocks she or he has chosen to represent each "problem," and to keep

them at all times, even while sleeping. One should carry the river rocks, well aware of their bulk and weight, until it is decided that they are no longer worth carrying. Anyone participating in this exercise should remember that the rocks represent "problems" which cannot just be put down until there is "good" reason for doing so.

PURIFICATION TECHNIQUES OF THE WEST: INDEPENDENCE

The West techniques are related to physical endurance and competition. Traditionally these were teachings for independence and a sense of equality. The techniques such as "the Mask" provide an opportunity for us to make or create a mask that describes how we feel. A traditional ceremony would be an opportunity when in the ceremonial dancing one would remove their mask to reveal themselves. The rest of the year they would try to live as themselves. Of course, things would happen that would create a mask to protect their feelings. This is a good exercise for children and adults.

Renaming is a way for us to "start anew by having a new name and being who we really want to be," says an elder, while we shake the stigma or negative feelings of the name we are using or that others used to call us. "Personal Distance" is an enjoyable activity with children and adults as we describe how much distance we want from others to feel comfortable. It is also used to describe safe distance from the energy influence of someone else or for people we work in groups. "The Bridge" is a "cross-over" experience where we can actually cross a bridge or visualize it as a way to balance ourselves as we feel what is going on inside of us as we get to the other side.

The Mask

The purpose of this exercise is to develop awareness of a person's present self-concept. We all have a mask that we wear at particular times, or even several masks for different situations.

Step 1: While gathered in the circle, the leader shares a brief background on the significance of masks for traditional use in ceremonies and everyday life.

Step 2: Participants are then asked to draw a mask that represents them either as they see themselves, as others see them, or as they would like to be seen. When everyone is finished, the participants rejoin the circle.

Step 3: Taking turns around the circle, each participant holds the mask over his or her face for a few moments. The person removes the mask to answer the following questions:

1. How do you see yourself? How would you describe yourself?

2. How do other people see you? How would others describe you?

3. How would you like to be seen?

Time for expressing thoughts and feelings is an important part of the mask exercise. Feedback from other group members may be useful. The mask can be saved as a reminder or destroyed as a "clearing-way."

Renaming

This exercise follows a tradition of renaming with words or thoughts that are more fitting to the person. The purpose here is to reveal the transitory nature of the words with which we or others may associate a certain worth that is truly independent of names. The realization will be created that we often let names dictate the worth of ourselves and others. Everyone is given a name at birth. However, the worth of something or someone can easily change in spite of the names associated with it; true worth is independent of words.

> **Step 1:** The exercise begins by having the members observe the names of animals, objects, or anything in their familiar environment. Focusing on these same items, participants are asked to generate names that are better fitting, or make us feel better about ourselves.

> **Step 2:** Participants are then encouraged to give themselves a name that is best-fitting. This could be based on a distinguishing characteristic, such as the name Tree for a very tall man, or some personal achievement or experience. The following questions can be used as a guideline:

> 1. If you could rename yourself with any word that best fits you as a person, what would it be?

> 2. What personal quality or experience makes you choose that name?

> **Step 3:** Time is devoted in the circle to a discussion of certain attributes represented by the new names and reasons for Renaming. Again, time is given for the expression of concerns or feelings that may arise. Names

are understood to only be valid for the duration of the session, though some may choose to retain new names privately as a reminder of personal strengths.

The purpose becomes that of helping members understand that their given names, especially the names given by others, do not necessarily represent their true selves. We can create disharmony in ourselves by allowing others to create disharmony in us. This can sometimes take the form of names.

Personal Distance

This is an exercise in body awareness, limit setting, and interpersonal respect. Every person has a preference for personal distance, that is, a distance that others keep in order for that individual to remain comfortable. We have all experienced having our personal distance violated and feeling a rising level of discomfort because of it; for example when someone bumps into us or stands too close. There are obvious social and cultural norms for what is considered appropriate distancing between people. However, there are many circumstances where we have little choice over distancing, as others violate our personal distance either knowingly or unknowingly. The Personal Distance exercise helps us to better understand why we feel uncomfortable with others who we do not know being too close to us. The usual distance for comfort is an arm's length. It is more comfortable to have about a foot of distance in sitting or standing next to another person while in a group. In earlier times of Sweat Lodge Ceremony it was important to have people who were comfortable with each other sit side by side during a sweat. It was better to have some people go into a sweat alone, because others felt uncomfortable next to them.

In a group where there are people who do not know each other, it is necessary for participants to get to know each other in an informal way to avoid a level of discomfort. This is always done in the beginning or before entrance in the "sweat." In the Full Circle gathering we use the smudge and relaxing drumming to calm any anxiety, so each person "is in their own world or comfort zone where they feel protected," as an elder put it. Do remember that touching someone should only happen with that person's permission and willingness to be touched.

Step 1: The leader asks for two volunteers and one is asked to stand with arms outstretched on both sides. Using the arms as a measure of personal distance, the participant is instructed to say "stop" when his or her personal distance is violated. The other person is asked to walk slowly toward the stationary person and stop when instructed to do so. The level of discomfort can be discussed by focusing on the stationary person's reactions to being in a somewhat awkward position. The moving person may also experiment with feelings of awkwardness by getting closer than his or her personal distance would normally permit.

Step 2: Afterward, the leader can repeat the process by assuming the role of the moving person and walking slowly toward the stationary person, stopping as directed. Then, to make a crucial point, the leader may unexpectedly touch the volunteer, for example on the shoulder, and ask for an honest reaction of comfort level. Respect for others can be discussed with the group at this point. The leader now repeats the previous actions but this time, asks for permission before touching the person. If the person asks not to be touched, the leader respects this request.

Step 3: The two volunteers can then switch positions and repeat the process to determine the other's personal distance. Everyone who wants to participate in the exercise should be allowed, in turn. Comparisons can be made between the varying personal distances of different people, always stressing the importance of asking permission and avoiding making unnecessary assumptions about others.

The Bridge

While this exercise can be used in any direction, the West or physical, is a very effective place for it. Traditional Indian elders taught that the future and the past are connected by a bridge that is especially critical during transition periods. Such periods include moving from childhood into the teens, then into early adulthood and on into becoming an elder. The Bridge is a visualization exercise used to focus on where we are at one end of the bridge and what is on the other side. The Bridge can also be used as a technique to face fears of the unknown and for reassurance that the "other side" is not death or an ending, but a new beginning.

Step 1: Participants can be taken to a bridge in a quiet environment or park, or if this is not possible the bridge can be visualized mentally. The exercise starts by having a participant on one end of the bridge. This person gently places water on his or her hands and face, giving thanks or reciting some expression of relaxation.

Step 2: The participant now slowly walks across the bridge until she or he finds a "safe" or quiet spot. The person stops at that spot and focuses on where she or he is before proceeding slowly to the other side. The process of moving from one side to the other while focusing on awareness is known as "cross-over."

Step 3: At the other side, the participant is allowed to relax and observe his or her inner thoughts. At that point, the experience can be written down or talked about in a coming-together.

In the Full Circle gathering we usually have participants divided into groups or clans who listen and lend support for whatever comes up in going over the actual bridge, or "Cross-Over." It is most often a measure of how well balanced we are. If something is bothering us, such as conflict with someone, as an example, there might be some emotional upset. Sometimes a person will cross the bridge not feeling anything, then suddenly feel down or feel something going on. The group will allow each person to share the experience, and a helper will be there to facilitate the sharing and clarifying. If necessary, the leader who is a counselor will be asked for clarification.

This technique is more effective with adults and the elderly. The experiences in the Full Circle gathering of "Cross-Over" range from not feeling anything but enjoying the experience to emotional outpouring. The experience gives us permission to feel and to open up to the energy blocks inside of us. No suggestions are given about the experience, except that it is all right to open up energy. This is similar to the exercise of open-hands/closed-hands, where opening the hands opens the energy flow. Each participant allows the distance at least of six feet from each other and "feels" if it is more comfortable to look upstream or downstream, as well as note where they are on the bridge as a comfortable spot.

An elder says, "Everything matters about how someone feels in the water [or crossing over the bridge]. The old ones would say that a preference for upstream is wanting to be in the rushing energy work, while downstream is moving out of the rushing energy." The most important point is what messages you receive when on the other side of the bridge and what emotional feelings or "voids" exist. In other words, are you open to letting stuff come out or are you continuing to deny feelings. Of course, one could be in total harmony and balance while just enjoying the experience and noticing other's experiences. There are many lessons to learn from such a simple activity.

PURIFICATION TECHNIQUES OF
THE NORTH: GENEROSITY

The North represents the direction of calm and wisdom for understanding. This includes generosity and understanding, such as teaching and sharing skills for survival in earlier years or sharing new ways to make things better for the tribe.

The purification ways of the North focus on ways to make things better or to improve life. The "Totem Exercise" helps us with personal power, while visualization of "The Mountain" exercise gives us permission to seek healing. "The Guide" and "The Sacred Path" provide meditations that allow us to find calm during conflict or just simple relaxation for healing. "Giveaway" is a sharing that can include gifting or simply thanking someone for their comments or contribution. It is reassuring and helps people feel that someone is interested in or concerned for them.

Totem Exercise

It is always important for us to remember our place in creation as one among many and to honor this truth. All things hold lessons for us to learn as we progress along our own sacred paths. Sometimes in order to better know ourselves and our own strengths we must take the time and patience to listen to the lessons presented to us by those things around us. It is believed that each of the animals of creation hold at least one lesson for us to learn. Each animal has its own "Medicine" or way of things, and in a sense, possesses its own unique personality. The same is obviously true of people. And for every person, there is at least one animal with which that person can identify. Gaining an understanding of the lesson held by a person's totem, or animal, carries with it a source of power and of healing for that person, which can be drawn upon at any time.

Step 1: The participant thinks of an animal that he or she identifies with or one that is most like him or her.

Step 2: Using the following questions, the connection between the individual and totem can be fully explored for a greater understanding of strengths and weaknesses.

1. Can you think of an animal with which you identify the most? What is it?

2. What are some things about you that are similar to this totem animal?

3. What is this animal's unique power according to its way of life?

4. What are some ways you can apply your own personal power using the lesson of your totem animal as a guide?

By making associations between the characteristics of the totem animal and the person, one's personal power can be discovered and used for purposes of healing and growth.

The Guide

The goal of this exercise is reflection for those who may be feeling overwhelmed or confused, or for anyone experiencing strong emotions. It has been used successfully for values clarification, or simply examining how one values an emotion or an experience in life and what it means to them. The guide can be that part of ourselves that can provide a message or answer to a problem. It can also be a way to call upon a spirit guide to help us with a conflict or decision in our lives. Often it helps to put our critical mind aside long enough to get an intuitive response.

Step 1: Participants are asked to create a personal guide in their mind. This should be someone whom they can consult in times of hardship or uncertainty. The guide can be an imaginary person or someone real, such as a respected elder, family member, or close friend. The guide should be well visualized as someone who stands beside the person, always available to offer words of wisdom or support.

Step 2: Participants are encouraged to take the time to consult their guide. Using the following questions, they consider how their guide might help them during a period of difficulty.

1. How would your guide see your situation?

2. What might your guide encourage you to do?

3. What would your guide's reasoning be for this course of action?

Step 3: Group members can serve as a resource by discussing their problem situations in turn with other members of the group.

With most decisions there is conflict within ourselves as to what we should do in making a decision. We go to a friend or someone we trust to help with the decision. In traditional teachings the Medicine Man would have the person "go to the mountain" or seek a vision or answer, knowing that somehow the Medicine Man would be there to guide the vision. This gave the person permission to seek the vision or answer and to be responsible with choice. Usually there was an answer or resolution that would sometimes require clarification or interpretation from the Medicine Man or Elder Priest. The confirmation by this elder would also reassure the person that he or she had the gift of intuition in making decisions, thereby reassuring of the choice and building confidence in personal decision making.

Giveaway

In traditional ceremonies the primary benefit of Giveaway is the sharing of gifts to honor special persons. It can also be an effective way to get rid of anger and clear memories that have caused grief and frustration. This technique emphasizes a person's decision-making ability to understand and release unnecessary burdens.

Writing a letter is similar to the traditional American Indian way of talking to your "power animal." The next step is to ask for guidance from a spirit guide on the issue shared.

Making a list is similar to the traditional idea of speaking about three or four (up to seven) things that are bothering you, out loud, for the "power animal" or "spirit guide" to hear the energy expressed outside of the body. It is a way express the feelings that are internal or to verbalize "what someone has conjured on you to make you feel harmed," as an elder said. "You cannot release it until you are able to give it away."

The clearing is to put this written expression of release into the sacred fire with tobacco to give thanks to the Great One.

Step 1: Following the example outlined below, the leader asks a participant to write a letter to him- or herself or to someone else describing an issue that is bothering him or her.

1. If you were to write a letter to _____, what might you say?

2. If you were to make a list about _____, what would it include?

Step 2: The person is then free to choose what to do with the letter—whether to save it, send it to the other person, tear it up into a million tiny pieces, or bury it in Mother Earth when she or he is ready to be done with it.

Instead of a healing-way for harmony, this is a way to balance the energy that has gotten out of balance due to conflict, "someone conjuring on you," or an event that has upset you. Being upset or having someone do something to interfere or influence you must be balanced with a clearing-way or Giveaway. The idea of "giving it up" to the sacred fire or burying it in Mother Earth clears it out and protects your energy. As the elder said, "We are most vulnerable when we are asleep or under the influence of alcohol or drugs. Under the influence is when a unwanted spirit can enter the body of a person, then it takes a Medicine Man [or Medicine Woman] to clear the spirit." The elder went on to say that sleep is a time when we can be scared or influenced by sudden noise, light, or other stimuli. The gift of tobacco to the fire or at the "moon time" (when it is full moon), or gifting tobacco to a creek or the ocean with a prayer of thanks to the Great One is a way to protect us from harm.

The teachings of "receptivity" in the North relate to vision seeking and calm meditation. It has much to do with what we have to share with others. First, we must be in harmony with our environment and all within the Universal Circle. This is the adult stage of life, where we know our "power animal" and are receptive to messages and guidance. "The Mountain" is for rest, reflection, and receptivity as we visit a place of vision seeking.

"The Sacred Path" would have traditionally been the sound of the drumming or flute to move us into a place where we are safe to feel. We focus on touch, sound, and feeling of nature. The key is to find a place of calm and healing. The traditional story is about the sacred lake of the North where we travel a path in the Four Directions to reach a place where we are guided into an enchanted area of abundance and safety. At that point we are in a place of receptivity and generosity, where we receive humbly and want to give to others what we have received. We are ready to share with others our gift of teaching, medicinal use of plants, skills as a hunter, or guidance to those in our tribe for survival in the Universal Circle of life.

The Mountain

A visit to the mountain is traditionally a way of seeking a vision. The quiet, sometimes cool environment and the calm of an elevated place are considered sacred. The birds and animals of the mountains represent a strength usually associated with adulthood. This exercise is a quest to find peace and quiet for meditation and vision seeking. Its primary purpose is to encourage inner seeking, expression of an inner vision, and a connection with Mother Earth and the surroundings such as the winds, the birds, and the sky.

For this exercise a leader goes with the participant to a mountain—either physically or mentally, using pictures and visualizations. A hike in the woods is very effective for this inner search. A calm and quiet environment is key for rest and reflection. Sitting under a tree and covering oneself with a shawl or blanket from the shoulders down provides a sense of protection from the wind and cool.

If we listen to what the elements have to tell us, recognizing similarities and differences, the wind, the birds, and the animals tend to become spiritual messages carrying the need for change in one's path, or simply a comforting presence. This is an excellent way for friends or support persons to involve themselves by accompanying the participant to the mountain in search of healing and wellness.

The Sacred Path

The Sacred Path is a powerful healing technique using guided imagery. The use of visualization and deep relaxation enables the participants to enter into a state of inner calm and peace.

Step 1: Begin by asking the participants to sit or lie in a comfortable position. Have them loosen any restricting clothing and instruct them to take some deep breaths to clear their minds and hearts as much as possible.

Step 2: Using any form of soothing music, the leader reads the following script out loud.

Close your eyes. Get comfortable. Picture where you live and imagine yourself there. Take all the feelings of stress and tension out of your body and leave them in a bag by the door. Now, imagine yourself leaving the area where you live. Leave the daily hassles and the struggles behind. Imagine yourself going across a valley, moving closer and closer to a mountain range. Breathe in the fresh air and the smell of grass as you go. Feel the warmth of the sun on your skin and relax with deep breathing.

Imagine yourself walking in the mountains now. You are going up a winding road. Off to one side, you can see the haze-covered mountains and the sky stretching on forever. Find a place on the winding road to stop. Listen to the rustling of leaves. Smell the cool mountain air. Take off your shoes if you want to and feel the earth under your feet. Feel the calmness all around you. Let the calm enter you like a breath of air . . .

Find a path leading away from the road, deeper into the forest. Start walking up the path. Take your time. Look at the animals as you go—they are your brothers and sisters, they are welcoming you into their homes. Look at the trees. Listen to what they are whispering . . .

Find a comfortable place on the path to stop. Listen to the echo of the birds singing. Feel the gentle breeze on your face. Nearby, you can hear the trickling waters of a stream. Keep walking up the path until you come to the stream . . .

When you have come to the stream, find a comfortable place to stop by the edge of the stream. Listen to the water trickling slowly. Bend down and dip your hands in the cool water, giving thanks to the water for its power and healing energy. Rub some of the water on your face and on your neck. Go ahead and step into the water if you want to. Feel its coolness on your skin . . .

Here, at this place, take some time to get rid of any stress and tension that is left in your body, in your mind, in your spirit. Take the stress and tension out of your body, out of your mind, out of your spirit. Look at it all very carefully and after you have done this, put it all down by edge of the stream. Ask Mother Earth to absorb it for you, and give thanks to her. Listen to the water for a few moments before moving on . . .

Now, continue walking up the path until you come to the top of the mountain. Walk through the deep woods, watching the sunlight flickering through the leaves as you move. Give thanks to the trees for offering their protection. When you come to the top of the mountain, look out over the mountain and observe everything stretching out before you in its greatness and beauty. What do you see? . . .

Find an inviting, comfortable place and go there. Be aware of your surroundings. Be aware of the calm and the feeling of this place. Touch things if you want to. Greet them with respect and honor their existence. This is your sacred place. It is part of you and you are part of it. What is your sacred place like? Be aware of all that you see, all that you smell, all that you hear, all that you feel. Be aware of how you are feeling. Get settled and gradually let the calm of this place become a part of you. Let the calm enter your body, your mind, your spirit like a breath—like the spirit of the Four Winds coming into you . . .

You are now feeling completely relaxed. You are safe here. Experience being relaxed, totally and completely. You are the calm . . .

Look around at your sacred place once more. Look at all the things that are around you here to protect and guide you. Feel the calm of this place and feel the calm that is inside you. Remember that this is your sacred place to seek the calm, and you can come here anytime you want. You are part of this place and it is part of you . . .

Slowly, come back to the room now. Keep the feeling of calm inside of you. Bring it with you. Slowly come back, and tell yourself that this is something you have created, and you can go to your sacred place whenever you want to feel the calm. When you have come back, open your eyes.

Allow plenty of time for working through what was seen, felt, and experienced remembering that "calm is healing."

12
The Full Circle Gift

An elder sat on a rock in the water at Collins Creek. The old name use to be "di ga da tla dv," or Arrow Creek. With him was a Natchez-Cherokee by the name of Archie Sams from Oklahoma. The Cherokee elder talked about the Four Winds or Powers that circle the Four Directions and the guidance through teachings from the Old Wisdom. These teachings were a gift from the Great One through the "apportioners," such as the Sun. He goes on to say, "We have lost too much, but what we know is a gift. We have been told by the ancestors that other things will come to us, and we will be renewed in our ways of survival like the people of old times."

The young ones chosen to learn are there to listen to the elders. Some of them want to write these things down, but that is not the way. Others focus on certain teachings, but one will get the message clearly and walk away with an understanding. This person is the teacher, or "keeper of the wisdom."

The Four Directions help to solidify the activities and exercises that are used to focus the teachings for everyone to enjoy and to learn a piece of the "Medicine," all that is sacred and special in life. In the Medicine of the Four Directions are these important questions:

East: Who or what are we a part of?

South: What do we enjoy doing that we do well?

West: What do we believe in as important?

North: What do we have to share with others?

The elders share stories, which are a way to recall and remember the sacred lessons that are sometimes in a story, a song, a dance, and possibly just a special place. Instead of intellectualizing and criticizing we learn to feel and hear on several different levels of learning. We know the presence of our ancestors are there as the spirits rush in and out like darts finding their target on the bull's eye. We feel struck by the "zapping" of the energy from the spirits present. Words are difficult to describe the feelings, but a humble attempt is made to make these connections:

East: Belonging and connectedness

South: Mastery and fun

West: Independence and introspection

North: Generosity and receptivity

The reader may say that some of these ideas are not explained in the book, and the author says that some things are left to the sacredness of the traditional wisdom. The activities are recalled because each of us will teach and guide others through one of the activities or exercises in each of the Four Directions. The reader has been gifted with the following:

East: I-Me, Switching, and the Friendship Circle

South: Mirroring, the Crazy Dog, and Split-Self Techniques

West: Mask, Renaming, Twelve Statement, and the Bridge

North: The Totem, the Guide, and Giveaway

Beyond the wisdom of the North are the visualization exercises that are taught in the North wisdom, but sometimes called the fifth direction or sacred way. These include "the Mountain" and "the Sacred Path."

We learn many things from these Four Directions ceremonies that help us to understand that the Fifth Ceremony relates to the sky and the stars, while the Sixth Ceremony is the lower world. It is sometimes even called the "turtle that holds the world up, which are held in place by sacred invisible cords in each of the Four Directions," as an elder explained. We celebrate the centrality of family in the East; the innocence of youth in the south; the strength of competition in the West; and the sharing of sacredness in the North. We understand that we are dimensional beings here for the purpose of being a helper to all living things and a protector of our Earth Mother.

We feel somehow gifted with this sharing and experience of Full Circle with a magical sense that there is much more. Yet, what more could we really comprehend or appreciate? We have understanding and wisdom that will truly help us to survive yesterday, today, and tomorrow. Our vision is our own and the way or path is of our own choice. We are guided, yet we come together in our own experience of life to the circle we call Full Circle. We do not join, but we are invited.

Every Full Circle ends as every ceremony ends, with the drumming coming to a close, with a traditional song-chant and a traditional Blessing-way. We know that this is not the end, but the beginning-again as we come Full Circle.

Wah Doh! (Sgi)

Our life purpose "crystallizes" when we gain enlightenment
about our connection with harmony and balance in life.
We are all connected.

For information on Full Circle gatherings please write to
J.T. and Michael Garrett in care of the publisher.

Inner Traditions • Bear & Company
P.O. Box 388
Rochester, VT 05767
1-800-246-8648
www.InnerTraditions.com

Or contact your local bookseller